It's Elementary
Special Topics in
Elementary Education

Patricia A. Crawford and
Kathleen Glascott Burriss, Editors

A C E I
Association for Childhood Education International
17904 Georgia Ave., Ste. 215, Olney, MD 20832
800-423-3563 • www.acei.org

Anne W. Bauer, ACEI Editor
Bruce Herzig, ACEI Editor
Deborah Jordan Kravitz, Production Editor

Copyright © 2002, Association for Childhood Education International
17904 Georgia Ave., Ste. 215, Olney, MD 20832

Library of Congress Cataloging-in-Publication Data
It's elementary!: special topics in elementary education / Patricia A. Crawford and
Kathleen Glascott Burriss, editors.
    p. cm.
Includes bibliographical references.
ISBN 0-87173-157-6 (pbk.)
    1. Elementary school teaching—United States. 2. Effective teaching—United States. I.
Crawford, Patricia A. II. Burriss, Kathleen Glascott.

LB1555 .I8 2002
372.1201—dc21

                                                        2002026027

Dedication

We dedicate this book to our parents:

James and Patricia Madden Crawford
Thomas and Marcella Glascott

With love and thanks for being our first teachers.

—PAC and KGB

Acknowledgments

Books are never created in a vacuum, and this one is no exception. We wish to acknowledge the hard work and significant contributions of the many people who helped to make this text a reality.

First and foremost, we thank the contributing authors for their thoughtful work and excellent writing. Clearly, this collection would not exist without their expertise and dedicated effort. We also thank the members of ACEI's Publications Committee. The idea for this book both sprang from and was nurtured by the committee. For this inspiration and support, we are most grateful. We wish to express appreciation for the thoughtful work of our reviewers: Robert Burke, Lauren Ventimiglia, and Sue Grossman. Their suggestions added to the quality of the collection. And, of course, we thank Anne Watson Bauer, ACEI's Director of Publications. Anne's editorial expertise has greatly enhanced our work, and her gracious leadership style has made it a joy to work on this project.

On a personal note, we thank those who have supported us in our writing endeavors. Trish especially thanks Patrick Shannon, Mary Jalongo, Kerry Crawford, and Jim Crawford, who all have been gracious mentors and fellow writers. Kathy wishes to fondly acknowledge the unfailing efforts of her husband, Larry, who by sharing his expertise as a journalist and educator has made her vision a reality.

—**Trish Crawford and Kathy Glascott Burriss**

Table of Contents

*Indicates a Focus on Elementary reprint.

Introduction

It's Elementary!
Special Topics in Elementary Education

Patricia A. Crawford,
University of Central Florida

Kathleen Glascott Burriss,
Middle Tennessee State University

"It's elementary!" This classic line, typically attributed to the fictional character Sherlock Holmes as directed to dear Watson, has become part of our vernacular. Although the statement cannot be found in the Sir Arthur Conan Doyle canon, it has become part of popular culture. Used in this manner, the term "elementary" communicates a sense of ease, signifying that the evidence has been laid out and the answer to a once-difficult puzzle now should be entirely obvious. "It's elementary!" is a way of saying that the issue at hand is a simple one that everyone should be able to understand and thus act upon.

While it is satisfying to have a good mystery story end with all of the evidence in place, all the loose ends tied up neatly, and all the issues brought to a close, such resolutions seldom occur in real life. In real life, evidence is often murky and its interpretation always influenced by situational specifics and matters of personal perspective. Complex situations mean that loose ends do and will abound, perspectives will differ to varying degrees, and complete closure on an issue is difficult to attain. In short, complexity makes for messiness and requires ongoing care and attention to the matters at hand.

Into the Classroom

This tension between simple, straightforward answers and the messiness of a complex social situation is evident within the world of education. On one hand, teaching is often viewed by the larger public as a simple task; one that easily could be performed by anyone with a bit of common sense. It seems that everyone—from policymakers to news reporters, and from politicians to parents—has strong opinions about the nature of formative education and what constitutes quality practices in schooling for children. This is not surprising, since most of the general population has had ongoing experiences within school systems—as students or parents of students (Shannon & Crawford, 1998; Weber & Mitchell, 1995).

People who work in education, as well as the general population, tend to base their ideas of model teachers and the proper construction of education on their own experience. Their memories of playing school, favorite classrooms, and good teachers, along with their impressions of "what worked in education," all contribute to a sense of "nostalgic expertise," which is enhanced by captivating, yet polarized, images of teachers in popular culture. Such notable fictional teachers as Mayberry's firm-but-fair Miss Krump, the Walton's kind-and-understanding Miss Hunter, the resistant-turned-inspiring Mr. Holland, and even the rough-but-loving drill sergeant from *Kindergarten Cop* have left indelible marks on our perceptions of what it means to be a teacher and work with the young (Shannon & Crawford, 1998). Mitchell and Weber (1999) note that the prevalence of educational themes in both popular culture and our own lives makes school "a veritable 'nostalgia factory' and thus [w]e are immersed in school outside of

9

school" (pp. 2-3).

With this mix of nostalgia and lived experience, teaching may seem like an act that is easily mastered—something that can be accomplished with a combination of kindness, good intentions, and listening to a few good tips from those around you. Insiders, however, know that this is a naïve perspective. Education is a complex and multi-layered domain, and teachers are required to balance numerous priorities. This is particularly true within the field of elementary education; elementary teachers work in a host of diverse settings, teach children across a variety of grades representing a wide range of developmental levels, and are responsible for content that spans all of the core subject areas and beyond.

In addition to these requirements, elementary teachers traditionally have been charged with a number of other important tasks. Responsibilities as diverse as nurturing the young, teaching basic skills, and preparing reflective, critical thinkers all fall under the domain of the elementary teacher. In many settings, teachers work to meet these goals in less than ideal circumstances and within institutional frameworks that are increasingly demanding; meanwhile, calls for education reform and increased accountability have become louder and more explicit than during any other time in recent memory. As teachers work diligently to educate and meet the many needs of the children entrusted to their care, it becomes clear that elementary teaching is challenging, demanding work. In short, elementary teaching is anything but elementary.

Purpose and Scope

This book was born out of the belief that members of ACEI and other interested readers would benefit from a special publication that addressed the needs of those teachers who define themselves as elementary-oriented. The purpose of this edited collection is to bring together a variety of pieces that address a range of topics and issues related to elementary education.

Like elementary education itself, the pieces in this collection are diverse and cover a wide range of topics. Although each chapter is discrete, the aim of each author was to address a particular topic by bringing together strong practical applications with well-grounded theory. The material for the chapters is drawn from two sources: reprints from ACEI's *Focus on Elementary Newsletter* and original works that were written especially for this collection. The chapters are organized around eight sectional themes relevant to the work of elementary teachers: *Celebrating Diversity, Classroom Configurations, Reading Revisited, Writing World, Content Connections, Today's Classroom, Artistic Avenues,* and *Assessment Alternatives.*

What's Elementary?

More than a quarter of a century ago, Herb Kohl (1976/1986) looked at the nature of our professional work in his now classic text, *On Teaching:*

Teaching is no simple matter. It is hard work, part craft, part art, part technique, part politics, and it takes time to develop ease within such a complex role. However, for many of us, the effort makes sense, for one gets the opportunity to see young people grow while one has a positive and caring role in their lives. (p. 13)

Kohl's words are just as significant today as they were at the time they first appeared. For those of us who work with elementary students and the teachers who teach them, "It's elementary!" will never mean that the work is simple or that we have all of the loose ends tied up neatly. Although elementary teaching will always be challenging, for us it makes sense because we see the potential in it to make a difference in both the lives of our students and in the broader sphere of society. We hope that this collection will be a good resource and one helpful tool among many for teachers to take on their journey.

References

Kohl, H. (1976/1986). *On teaching.* New York: Schocken.

Mitchell, C., & Weber, S. J. (1999). *Education and popular culture.* New York: Teachers College Press.

Shannon, P., & Crawford, P. (1998). Summers off: Representations of teachers' work and other discontents. *Language Arts, 75,* 255-264.

Weber, S. J., & Mitchell, C. (1995). *That's funny, you don't look like a teacher! Interrogating images and identity in popular culture.* London: Falmer.

Celebrating Diversity

Chapter 1
Fifteen Misconceptions About Multicultural Education

Jerry Aldridge,
University of Alabama at Birmingham

Charles Calhoun,
University of Alabama at Birmingham

Ricky Aman,
Cal-Tex, Pekanbaru, Sumatra, Indonesia

The movement toward multicultural education has gained momentum over the past 20 years. Guidelines from professional organizations have been in place for some time. While many elementary educators support multicultural development and genuinely try to incorporate diverse cultural issues into the curriculum, some widespread misconceptions about what multicultural education is and how it should be implemented hinder the process. Specifically, at least 15 common misconceptions should be addressed:

1. People from the same nation or geographic region, or those who speak the same language, share a common culture. At least seven distinct dialects and cultures can be found in the Southern United States alone (Cross & Aldridge, 1989). Most Latinos share a common language, but they cannot be considered as one ethnic group sharing a similar culture; they may also speak in many different dialects. Tremendous historical, racial, and cultural differences must be acknowledged (Banks & Banks, 1997). The cultures of Cuba, Mexico, Puerto Rico, and Argentina are distinctly different from one another, even though they share the same language. In Canada, the language (French

Canadian) and culture of Quebec vary dramatically from that of Alberta and other provinces (Aldridge & Goldman, 2002).

Numerous similar examples in Asia also can be found. In Indonesia, for example, while many people speak Bahasa Indonesian, the country is actually home to hundreds of different languages and dialects and numerous diverse cultures. One can find Sundanese, Bataks, Minang, Javanese, Balinese, Dayak, Toraja, and the many tribal languages and cultures of Irian Jaya. In Malaysia, there are Malays, Chinese, East Indians, and the tribal groups of Sarawak. To view regions or nations as if they were monocultural is erroneous, and it may inhibit students' construction of the fact that many parts contribute to the whole.

2. Families from the same culture share the same values. This notion is especially false for nondominant cultures living in the United States. Lynch and Hanson (1998) reported at least four ways individuals and families from other countries "live out" their culture in the United States. These include "1) mainstreamers, 2) bicultural individuals, 3) culturally different individuals, and 4) culturally marginal individuals" (p. 19). In reality, a continuum of cultural identity exists and the entire range often can be found within the same family. For example, grandparents may maintain their original culture, while their grandchildren may be bicultural or mainstreamers.

3. *Children's books about another culture are usually authentic.* This is an especially common misconception. Teachers who want to share other cultures may unintentionally choose books that are racist or not representative of a particular group. Many of us can identify certain culturally inappropriate books, such as *The Story of Little Black Sambo* by Bannerman (1899), *The Five Chinese Brothers* by Bishop and Wiese (1939), or *The Seven Chinese Brothers* by Mahy (1990). The stereotypes in other books are more subtle. For example, one book that is often recommended (see Huck, Hepler, & Hickman, 1987) is *Tikki Tikki Tembo* (Mosel, 1968). The book does have a delightful repetitive pattern that many children enjoy. The text and illustrations, however, inaccurately depict Chinese people. In the text, the first and most honored son has the grand long name of "Tikki tikki tembo-no sa rembo-chari bari ruchi-pip peri pembo." The message about Chinese names is less than flattering. People in the Southern United States would be appalled if parents in the People's Republic of China were reading stories to their children about Southerners who used to give their children such names as Bubba Bubba Jimbo Kenny Ray Billy Bob.

In 1980, the Council on Interracial Books for Children published *Guidelines for Selecting Bias-Free Textbooks and Storybooks* (see Derman-Sparks, 1989). The guidelines suggest: 1) checking illustrations for stereotypes or tokenism, 2) checking the story line, 3) looking at the lifestyles (watching out for the "cute-natives-in-costumes" syndrome, for example), 4) weighing relationships between people, 5) noting the heroes, 6) considering the effect on a child's self-image, 7) considering the author's or illustrator's background, 8) examining the author's perspective, 9) watching for loaded words, and 10) checking the copyright date.

Other criteria are available to readers. For example, Rudine Sims Bishop (1993) has published guidelines in *Teaching Multicultural Literature in Grades K-8.*

4. *Multicultural education just includes ethnic or racial issues.* While ethnic and racial concerns are a large part of multicultural education, gender and socioeconomic diversity are also important. Children come from many types of homes, including those headed by lesbian or gay parents. Furthermore, people from lower socioeconomic status environments often have more in common with one another than they do with those of a similar racial or ethnic heritage, but from higher income levels (Strevy & Aldridge, 1994).

One source that is helpful in dispelling this myth is *Teaching With a Multicultural Perspective: A Practical Guide* (Davidman & Davidman, 1997). Sleeter and Grant (1993) also have written extensively about school goals for multicultural education. These include the promotion of "equal opportunity in the school, cultural pluralism, alternative life styles, and respect for those who differ and support for power equity among groups" (p. 171).

Gollnick and Chinn (1990) recommend five goals for multicultural education. These goals also emphasize issues beyond the boundaries of ethnic or racial issues. They include: 1) the promotion of strength and value of cultural diversity, 2) an emphasis on human rights and respect for those who are different from oneself, 3) the acceptance of alternative life choices for people, 4) the promotion of social justice and equality for all people, and 5) an emphasis on equal distribution of power and income among groups.

5. *The tour and detour approaches are appropriate for teaching multicultural education.* What are the tour and detour approaches? Louise Derman-Sparks (1993) uses the phrase "tourist multiculturalism" to describe approaches that merely *visit* a culture. The tour approach to education involves a curriculum that is dictated primarily by months or seasons of the year. For example, some teachers believe an appropriate time to study Native Americans is November, when Thanksgiving occurs in the United States. Elementary teachers may *take a detour* during November and have children make Indian headbands or present a Thanksgiving play. Simi-

larly, Black History Month often is the only time children study African American leaders or read literature written by black authors. Maya Angelou once remarked that she will be glad when Black History Month is no longer necessary. When all Americans are sufficiently a part of our courses of study and daily instruction, there will be no need for a black history week or month.

These tour and detour methods *trivialize, patronize,* and *stereotype* cultures by emphasizing traditional costumes, foods, and dances while avoiding the true picture of the *everyday life of the people* from that culture (Derman-Sparks, 1993). Students often come away from such teaching with even more biases. White students in one district checked out of school during a Black History Month program. Their parents explained that they felt "this program was for them—not us."

6. *Multicultural education should be taught as a separate subject.* Just as touring and detouring are not recommended practices, neither is teaching multicultural education as a separate subject. In fact, this is just another detour. In a subtle way, it points out that many groups are still on the margin of society.

James Banks (1994) has divided multicultural curriculum reform into four approaches: 1) the contributions approach, 2) the additive approach, 3) the social action approach, and 4) the transformation approach. This fourth approach is particularly powerful in addressing the myth of teaching multicultural education as a separate subject. In a transformation approach, the structure and basic assumptions of the curriculum are changed so that students can view concepts, issues, events, and themes from the perspectives of diverse ethnic and cultural groups. History often is written from the winner's perspective, and so in traditional curricula students only get to hear the voice of the victor. In a transformation approach, "students are able to read and listen to voices of the victors and the vanquished" (p. 26).

Making multicultural education a separate topic would simply add something else to teachers' already full plates. We advocate an approach that promotes education that is multicultural overall.

Multicultural concepts should be infused throughout the curriculum.

7. *Multicultural education is an accepted part of the curriculum.* In fact, this is far from true. There are current efforts to eliminate multicultural education from the schools. The popular media also has its staunch critics of multicultural education. On the back cover of Rush Limbaugh's (1994) popular book *See, I Told You So* he says, "Multicultural education is just an excuse for those who have not made it in the American way." It is important to note, however, that there has never been only one American culture, but many. Ross Perot used the term "melting pot" throughout his presidential campaigns. Perhaps a better way to look at the United States would be as a salad bowl (Aldridge, 1993). Unique, different cultures contribute to the whole country, just as a tomato or celery adds to the salad.

8. *Multiculturalism is divisive.* According to this myth, immigrants coming to the United States eventually will be assimilated and consider themselves as Americans. The myth goes on to state that when ethnicity is turned into a defining characteristic, it promotes division rather than unity. This shallow reasoning denies the multiple diversities that always have existed and continue to exist throughout the United States (Swiniarski, Breitborde, & Murphy, 1999).

9. *In predominantly monocultural or bicultural societies, there is no need to study other cultures.* This myth is pervasive in such societies. For example, we have heard some undergraduate education students protest, "Why should we study other cultures when there are only whites and blacks in the class and in our community?" In the past two years, however, that same community has had an influx of Mexican and Asian families. Furthermore, the closest elementary school to the students who made this comment had 71 different nationalities represented in its student population. With an increasingly diverse society, bicultural and monocultural areas especially need to learn about cultures to which they will be in close proximity in the immediate future (Greenfield & Cocking, 1994).

10. Multicultural education should be reserved for older children who are less egocentric or ethnocentric. Lynch and Hanson (1998) tell us that "cultural understanding in one's first culture occurs early and is typically established by age 5" (p. 24). They go on to explain that "children learn new cultural patterns more easily than adults" (p. 25). Young children are capable of learning that we are all alike and all different in certain ways. Children in the early elementary grades often study the family and community. Gathering pictures of each family and discussing the differences and similarities is a good place to start. Interestingly enough, the critics who suggest that multicultural education should be postponed are often the same ones who are interested in pushing academics down into the preschool curriculum.

11. When multicultural education is implemented, the commonality is lost (Swiniarski, Breitborde, & Murphy, 1999). As school curricula expand to incorporate more diverse cultures, conflicts may arise just as they did with the civil rights movement. However, multicultural education can assist society in being more tolerant, inclusive, and equitable, helping people recognize that the whole is rich with many contributing parts (see Ravitch, 1991/1992).

12. Americans do not need multicultural education because they already acknowledge cultural diversity. Those who agree with this statement are quick to point out that Martin Luther King's birthday and Black History Month are widely celebrated. This is exactly what we mean by a tour or detour approach, which is often more divisive than transformative (see Derman-Sparks, 1989).

13. Historical accuracy suffers in multicultural education. Proponents of this statement have suggested that certain curricula promote that Cleopatra was black and that western civilization started in Egypt rather than Greece. If students are taught appropriate skepticism at an early age, then they will develop questioning abilities to research discrepancies found in historical literature (Greenfield & Cocking, 1994).

14. Most people identify with only one culture. Increasingly, children and families are multiethnic in nature. Here are just two examples. Maria is an Evangelical Christian from Ecuador who married Mohammed, a Muslim from Pakistan. They have two elementary-age children who are being raised in Queens, New York. The children have never visited Ecuador or Pakistan. Patrick is of Chinese heritage, but was born in Jamaica. His family later moved to Toronto and now lives in Miami.

These children are not stereotypical. They each have a unique cultural heritage. Multicultural education should examine intrapersonal, as well as interpersonal, cultural diversity. If this is not acknowledged and valued, children like Patrick could experience intrapsychic cultural conflict.

15. Finally, there are not enough resources available about multicultural education. Nothing could be further from the truth. In fact, in the past 10 years, a plethora of sources has emerged concerning cultural diversity. We have found the references in this article to be very helpful. The list of multicultural Web sites provided at the end of this article offers other valuable resources for elementary teachers.

There are, no doubt, many other misconceptions about multicultural education. These 15 represent those encountered in the authors' personal experiences. Although all three authors of this chapter come from different races, cultural backgrounds, and religions, we are sometimes surprised at our own lack of understanding and by some of our own misconceptions that we have constructed in the past. As have many teachers, we have participated in some of these myths. However, we have a commitment to multicultural education and learning. As we continue to examine our own misconceptions about diversity, we hope you will make the effort to do the same.

References

Aldridge, J. (1993). *Self-esteem: Loving yourself at every age.* Birmingham, AL: Doxa.

Aldridge, J., & Goldman, R. (2002). *Current issues and trends in education.* Boston: Allyn & Bacon.

Banks, J. (1994). *An introduction to multicultural education.* Needham Heights, MA: Allyn & Bacon.

Banks, J., & Banks, C. (Eds.). (1997). *Multicultural education: Issues and perspectives* (3rd ed.). Boston: Allyn & Bacon.

Bannerman, H. (1899). *The story of Little Black Sambo.* New York: HarperCollins.

Bishop, C., & Wiese, K. (1939). *The five Chinese brothers.* New York: Sandcastle.

Bishop, R. S. (1993). Multicultural literature for children: Making informed choices. In V. J. Harris (Ed.), *Teaching multicultural literature in grades K-8.* Norwood, MA: Christopher-Gordon.

Cross, K., & Aldridge, J. (1989). Introducing Southern dialects to children through literature. *Reading Improvement, 26*(1), 29-32.

Davidman, L., & Davidman, P. (1997). *Teaching with a multicultural perspective: A practical guide* (2nd ed.). New York: Longman.

Derman-Sparks, L., & the ABC Task Force. (1989). *Antibias curriculum: Tools for empowering young children.* Washington, DC: National Association for the Education of Young Children.

Derman-Sparks, L. (1993). Revisiting multicultural education: What children need to live in a diverse society. *Dimensions of Early Childhood, 22*(1), 6-10.

Gollnick, D., & Chinn, P. (1990). *Multicultural education in a pluralistic society* (3rd ed.). New York: Macmillan.

Greenfield, P., & Cocking, R. (Eds.). (1994). *Cross-cultural roots of minority child development.* Hillsdale, NJ: Lawrence Erlbaum Associates.

Huck, C., Hepler, S., & Hickman, J. (1987). *Children's literature in the elementary school* (4th ed.). New York: Holt, Rinehart and Winston.

Limbaugh, R. (1994). *See, I told you so.* New York: Simon and Schuster.

Lynch, E., & Hanson, M. (Eds.). (1998). *Developing cross-cultural competence: A guide for working with children and their families* (2nd ed.). Baltimore: Paul H. Brookes.

Mahy, M. (1990). *The seven Chinese brothers.* New York: Scholastic.

Mosel, A. (1968). *Tikki Tikki Tembo.* New York: Henry Holt and Compnay.

Ravitch, D. (1991/1992). A culture in common. *Educational Leadership, 49*(4), 8-11.

Sleeter, C., & Grant, C. (1993). *Making choices for multicultural education: Five approaches to race, class, and gender* (2nd ed.). New York: Macmillan.

Strevy, D., & Aldridge, J. (1994). Personal narrative themes of African American mothers. *Perceptual and Motor Skills, 78*, 1143-1146.

Swiniarski, L., Breitborde, M., & Murphy, J. (1999). *Educating the global village: Including the young child in the world.* Upper Saddle River, NJ: Merrill/Prentice Hall.

Multicultural Web Sites

In SITE — Multicultural Education: http://curry.edschool.virginia.edu

Multicultural Education Abstracts: www.carfax.co.uk

Multicultural Education: www.fau.edu

Center for Multilingual Multicultural Research: www-rcf.usc.edu/~cmmr

Multicultural Education: www.library.unt.edu

Chapter 2
Creating Caring Classroom Communities:
At the Heart of Education

Mary Little,
University of Central Florida

> *"Students will not*
> *care how much you know,*
> *until they know how*
> *much you care."*
>
> *—Anonymous*

At the heart of democracy is the belief that learning and education are the great equalizers of the human condition. It is through a free and appropriate education that each and every person realizes his or her potential as a successful, contributing member of society. Today, the challenges on the way to meeting this goal have increased in number and complexity. Since classroom communities are a subset of society as a whole, they often reflect current trends, needs, concerns, and promises. The societal concerns reported on the evening news can have names and faces the very next day in our classrooms.

School often is the vehicle used to address the needs of our youngest citizens. For education to be the true equalizer within a society, schools will likely be asked to address even more of these challenges. As a result, the concept of "education" has broadened in scope much beyond the traditional pursuit of academic excellence for all children. Education must be reconceptualized to meet the changing needs of our children, while keeping in mind that certain basic needs must be met before achievement and mastery can be attained (Maslow, 1970).

The focus of this article is to challenge educators' current thinking about teaching. In light of what is currently known about children and their basic needs, what are educators' responsibilities? Finally, a model for creating caring classroom communities will be shared as a means to address these changing needs.

Basic Needs and the Current Condition

Abraham Maslow (1970) developed a hierarchy of basic human needs (see Figure 1). The need for physiological basics (food, clothing, and shelter), safety, and a sense of belonging and love are the foundation of this hierarchy. Once these foundational needs are met, individual achievement and mastery (self-esteem) can be realized, leading to the ultimate goal of self-actualization. Current brain research supports the theory that the brain's automatic system of response, "fight or flight," will take over to protect an individual during times of perceived adversity (Hart, 1983). In other words, it is difficult, if not neurologically impossible, to engage in intellectual pursuits when the most basic needs are unmet.

Given this knowledge, the well-documented reports of children going without such basic necessities should shock our social consciousness (see Figure 2). As Marian Wright Edelman of the Children's Defense Fund concluded,

Millions of children are not safe physically, education-ally, economically, or spiritually. The poor black youths who shoot up drugs on street corners and the rich white youths who do the same thing in their mansions share a common disconnectedness from any hope or purpose. (Edelman, 1989, p. 24)

In addition, even schools, which once were considered safe havens, are facing safety concerns, as well as controversy about educational practices and academic achievement levels (Kozol, 1991).

Educators frequently argue that these societal issues are greater than the scope of "education" within the schools. Previously, children's basic needs were met primarily outside of the classroom by family, place of worship, and the community. Children entered schools "ready to learn." With so many of these needs not being met outside of the schools, however, educators are feeling the burden of raised expectations and many are feeling overwhelmed. Obviously, educators cannot cure all of society's woes. But, what *are* their responsibilities? How does the profession respond to the changing needs of children? These discussions are critical. In light of what we currently know, we must continue to define the roles and responsibilities of school within the context of a changing society. The author hopes

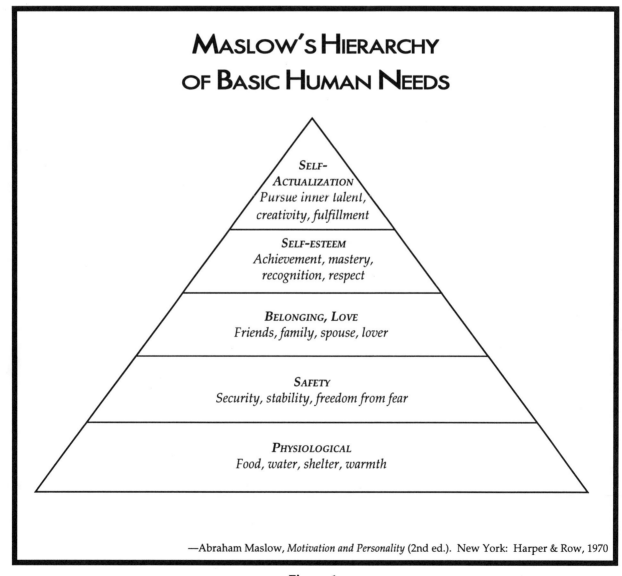

MASLOW'S HIERARCHY OF BASIC HUMAN NEEDS

SELF-ACTUALIZATION
Pursue inner talent, creativity, fulfillment

SELF-ESTEEM
Achievement, mastery, recognition, respect

BELONGING, LOVE
Friends, family, spouse, lover

SAFETY
Security, stability, freedom from fear

PHYSIOLOGICAL
Food, water, shelter, warmth

—Abraham Maslow, *Motivation and Personality* (2nd ed.). New York: Harper & Row, 1970

Figure 1

to fuel this discussion among educators, and to challenge current thinking about these issues, by presenting some facts and suggestions.

Current Responses

Responses to the changing needs of children, and the resulting expectations for educators, depend upon an accurate assessment of the problem within either a reactive or proactive frame of reference. Historically, educators have tended to attribute problems to the individual by labeling and assigning blame, and then combating or disengaging from the individual and the problem. Brendtro, Brokenleg, and van Bockern (1990) discussed professionals' common responses to the difficult challenges presented by youth—identifying, labeling (e.g., using descriptors such as "disturbed," "deprived," "dysfunctional," "disabled," etc.), and segregating—all in the name of treating the problem.

Eventually, these reactive responses actually created among children a greater sense of inferiority, while further exacerbating the problem by weakening their sense of belonging. This led to children feeling more rejected and discouraged and being increasingly disrespectful (Brendtro, Brokenleg, & van Bockern, 1990). Kunc (1992) suggests that responding to students' poor behavior by suspending or expelling them actually corrupts Maslow's hierarchy of basic needs. These reactive responses demand that children attain achievement, mastery, and positive recognition *before* the children may belong to, and be included in, the class or in the school.

Proactively Meeting Basic Needs

Proactive planning and implementation of educational responses that address basic needs can best counteract reactive responses. Principles of healthy child development that have developed across disciplines and centuries (Coopersmith, 1967; Glasser, 1986; Mendler, 1992) focus on four specific human needs: connection, competence, self-control, and contribution.

The first of the basic needs is a sense of belonging and *connection* within a group. Significance is

---

SIGNS OF STRESS & ALIENATION IN THE UNITED STATES

Every Day in America . . .

1 young person under 25 dies from HIV infection.

5 children or youth under 20 commit suicide.

9 children or youth under 20 are homicide victims.

9 children or youth under 20 die from firearms.

34 children and youth under 20 die from accidents.

77 babies die.

157 babies are born at very low birthweight (less than 3 lbs., 4 oz.).

180 children are arrested for violent crimes.

367 children are arrested for drug abuse.

401 babies are born to mothers who had late or no prenatal care.

825 babies are born at low birthweight (less than 5 lbs., 8 oz.).

1,310 babies are born into families without health insurance.

1,329 babies are born to teen mothers.

2,019 babies are born into poverty.

2,319 babies are born to mothers who are not high school graduates.

*2,861 high school students drop out.**

3,585 babies are born to unmarried mothers.

4,248 children are arrested.

7,883 children are reported abused or neglected.

17,297 public school students are suspended.

* Based on calculations per school day
(180 days of seven hours each).

© 2002 Children's Defense Fund

Figure 2

found through acceptance, attention, and the affection of others (Coopersmith, 1967). *Competence* develops as one masters the environment (i.e., successfully masters the academic and behavioral content and expectations at school). Success brings innate satisfaction and a sense of efficacy, while chronic failure stifles motivation (Coopersmith, 1967). The ability to control one's own behavior, and therefore gain others' respect, helps children develop a sense of control, power, and independence. This *self-control* and resulting power counteract the negative feelings of helplessness and resultant external locus of control (e.g., the tendency to say "It's not my fault!"). As children make a *contribution*, through generosity and giving to others, they build a sense of worthiness. Without feelings of worthiness, life is not fulfilling.

Although some of these issues appear daunting, Covey (1991) suggests that any proactive action plan must begin within our circle of influence. Teachers possess tremendous opportunities to significantly and permanently affect children's development (Ginott, 1990). In fact, the very nature of the major concerns facing our children today depends upon teachers' influences. Effective schools are often characterized by a proactive, caring school community, rather than a series of isolated practices in reaction to current perceived problems (Phi Delta Kappa Commission on Discipline, 1982). Educational institutions serve as powerful environments through which to transmit societal values, norms, and social mores to the young (Wozner, 1985). But how do we proactively plan and create a caring school community that addresses the basic needs for healthy child development?

Framework for Change

Based upon the four basic developmental needs for all children, the Community Circle of Caring model (Blankstein & DuFour, 1997) was created to provide a specific framework for change. Through the concepts of connection, competence, self-control, and contribution, educators can create caring classroom and school communities that address students' basic developmental needs.

The first component for change is to create a *connection* for students. It is said that people want to be connected with something larger, more identifiable, and more important than them. Whether as members of a street gang or a church choir, an affiliation and connection to a group begins by being welcomed. From the very first day of class, it is critical to include all students as connected members of the total group. Do we spend the time to connect the students with the adults in the school and classroom, and with the other students? Is there at least one other person who is connected to each of the students? Are the special talents and interests of each member of the class discovered and enhanced within the group? Are identifiable emblems or signs visible to the members of the class or activity group? Is every member of the class or school valued as a person?

Second, it is said that information is power. Within a classroom, *competence* at academic tasks is critical. Competence in the information and objectives of a particular curriculum provides the power of knowledge. Is each student mastering the curriculum? What strategies and techniques have been implemented to plan for student learning? Teachers must consider the full variety of instructional techniques to help develop each child's competence. The use of certain techniques, such as cooperative learning, mnemonics, advance organizers, active engagement strategies, and peer tutoring, enhances the competence for each student within the classroom. Furthermore, schoolwide strategies, such as after-school tutoring, academic knowledge bowls, learning resource centers, and teacher assistance teams, also can enhance students' competence.

Teaching students to be responsible and to exercise *self-control* does not mean that students should be merely obedient (Kounin, 1970). Clearly organized and well-communicated expectations and procedures enhance student self-control within the classroom community. Explicitly articulating and reinforcing mutually agreed upon rules and roles for all members of the classroom community provide ownership and a sense of empowerment. Individual growth and continued contribution can occur once the framework for specific expectations has been agreed upon and communicated. Do students understand the expectations? Have the procedures been practiced and reinforced? Is the classroom well-organized, so as to maximize the teaching and learning process? Have the students had an active role in the development of the classroom and school procedures? Are there natural consequences within the community?

Finally, engaging and effective classroom communities enhance the *contributions* of all members (Little, 1997). By knowing each student's strengths, interests, and needs, a teacher can engage students more actively. By employing various active engagement techniques (e.g., questioning skills, peer partners, classwide peer tutoring, variety of response methods), teachers can increase students' chances of success. Within the school, connecting each student with any one of numerous school-based activities will increase the opportunity for each student to make a positive contribution to the total school community.

Final Thoughts

Teaching continues to be one of the greatest responsibilities in society, and an opportunity to truly affect future generations. By taking proactive steps and planning to make at least one or two changes within classroom societies, each of us helps solve some of the problems facing all of us.

References

Blankstein, A., & DuFour, R. (1997). *Reaching today's students: Building the community circle of caring.* Bloomington, IN: National Educational Service.

Brendtro, L., Brokenleg, M., & van Bockern, S. (1990). *Reclaiming youth at risk: Our hope for the future.* Bloomington, IN: National Educational Service.

Coopersmith, S. (1967). *The antecedents of self-esteem.* New York: Perennial Library.

Covey, S. (1991). *Principle-centered leadership.* New York: Simon & Schuster.

Edelman, M. W. (1989). Children at risk. *Proceedings of the Academy of Political Science, 27*(2), 20-30.

Ginott, H. (1990). *Teacher and child.* New York: Simon & Schuster.

Glasser, W. (1986). *Control theory in the classroom.* New York: Harper & Row.

Hart, L. (1983). *Human brain and human learning.* New York: Longman.

Kozol, J. (1991). *Savage inequalities.* New York: Crown.

Kounin, J. (1970). *Discipline and group management in classrooms.* New York: Holt, Rinehart, and Winston.

Kunc, N. (1992). *The corruption of Maslow's hierarchy.* New York: Axis Consultation and Training.

Little, M. (1997). *Teaching our students: Building a community circle of caring.* Bloomington, IN: National Educational Service.

Maslow, A. (1970). *Motivation and personality.* New York: Harper & Row.

Mendler, A. (1992). *What do I do when...? How to achieve discipline with dignity in the classroom.* Bloomington, IN: National Educational Service.

Phi Delta Kappa Commission on Discipline. (1982). *Handbook for developing schools with good discipline.* Bloomington, IN: Author.

Wozner, Y. (1985). Institution as community. *Child and Youth Services, 7,* 71-90.

Chapter 3
In the Gap:
Bridging the Generations Through Literature and Learning Experiences

Patricia A. Crawford,
University of Central Florida

*"It was a flop—
nothing but a flop."*

These were the words a first-year teacher used to describe a lesson based on *Love You Forever*, Robert Munsch's (1986) well-known children's story that depicts the tender relationship between parent and child, while at the same time portraying the powerful emotions that often accompany the aging process. The emotional story tugs on more than a few heartstrings as it follows a mother and her son across the years—until they reach the point at which the parent is quite elderly and the child is an adult. Suddenly, their caregiving roles are reversed. The love remains constant, yet the relationship has changed. The text invites readers to explore the ways in which our own lives and relationships are transformed through the aging process.

This particular teacher loved Munsch's book, and was sure her 2nd-grade class would thoroughly enjoy the read aloud, be moved by the storyline, and work enthusiastically on an extension project that celebrated the older adults in their lives. She never got past the read aloud, however. The children giggled at illustrations she considered poignant. They described the characters' actions, which she found touching, as "silly" and "make believe." "Worst of all," the teacher reported, "they just didn't get it. They didn't understand

that the story was about love between generations. It didn't make them sad. They didn't even like the old lady. The whole lesson was a flop."

The teacher's experience raises several important questions. The first questions concern aging itself. What do children need to know about the aging process? What is the best way to facilitate this learning? How can educators help students develop informed perspectives and respond sensitively to the issue of what it means to grow old? The second group of questions concerns the audience of children's books that address aging and other sensitive issues. Are these texts really written for children, or are they intended primarily for adult enjoyment? Is it reasonable to expect children's responses to these stories to be similar to those of more mature readers? Finally, curricular questions need to be addressed. Should a lesson be considered a failure simply because students respond differently than anticipated? How can lessons such as these be transformed into valuable learning experiences?

Coming of Age
It is no surprise that America is graying (Blunk & Williams, 1997; Pipher, 1999; Smith & Newman, 1993). Demographics indicate that the number of Americans over the age of 65 doubled in the last 40 years of the 20th century, and projections indicate that this figure will double again in the first 40 years of the 21st century (U.S. Census Bureau, 1999). Also, during the last quarter of the 20th

century, the number of people over age 85 expanded at six times the rate of the general population growth of the United States, and centenarians (those citizens 100 years old or older) are one of the fastest-growing segments of the population (Carter, 1998). These startling figures provide good news for a society in which, only a century ago, the average life span was merely 46 years. It seems clear that the U.S. population has come of age. Therefore, it is essential that children develop a good understanding of the aging process, and that they have an informed perspective of what it means to be an older adult.

Beyond such facts and figures, there are important reasons for addressing age-related issues in the elementary school. First and foremost, aging is something that promises to affect children's lives in a personal and significant way. Young children interact with grandparents and with other older relatives, neighbors, and friends. They will witness their parents' aging process and will one day grow old themselves. Aging is a natural part of the human life cycle, one that brings both rewards and challenges. Therefore, it is important for children to have a balanced and informed perspective that allows them to sort through myths and stereotypes, develop positive self-concepts, and participate fully in healthy, enriching, and joyful cross-generational relationships.

Finally, research indicates that even young children tend to exhibit an anti-aging bias. That is, children at the preschool and elementary levels frequently associate negative characteristics with older adults, and they often state that they do not want to grow old themselves (Blunk & Williams, 1997; Seefeldt, Warman, Jantz, & Galper, 1990). These children are exhibiting the first signs of ageism, a belief that people "cease to be people, cease to be the same people, or become people of a distinct and inferior kind, by virtue of having lived a specific number of years" (Comfort, 1976, p. 35). Ageism is the systematic stereotyping of older adults, a form of prejudice not unlike that of racism or sexism (Carter, 1998). Ageist perspectives affect both the elderly and those who stereotype them. Therefore, it is essential that teachers take an anti-bias approach and address age-related issues in lessons, literature, and learning experiences.

Into the Classroom

Teachers can interrupt the cycle of age-related bias by creating a classroom atmosphere that is inclusive and supportive of all people, including older adults. To this end, classroom bulletin boards and displays should include representations of diverse groups of people (Derman-Sparks & the ABC Task Force, 1989). These collections should include images of older adults from a variety of cultural backgrounds, showing them actively involved in a full range of activities. Although it is fine to include traditional images (e.g., grandmothers who bake, grandfathers who fish), these displays also should include representations of adults engaged in experiences that challenge stereotypical notions (older adults gainfully employed, serving in the community, engaged in the arts, participating in athletic activities, etc.).

Teachers also can help elementary students develop accurate and informed perspectives of the aging process by inviting them to explore and celebrate the lives of older adults. On a broad level, students can study people who have made significant contributions in their later years. On a local level, students can examine newspapers and accounts of local events to identify older adults who are actively involved in their communities, and who are making a difference. Finally, on a personal level, students can celebrate the older people in their own lives. They can bring in pictures of older relatives, neighbors, and family friends. Social studies, literacy, and art concepts can be integrated in the curriculum, as students interview these people, document oral histories, write biographical pieces, and publish information related to their learning.

Beyond the Walls

Intergenerational studies provide a wonderful opportunity to extend learning beyond the classroom walls. Older community members can help bridge the gap between school and community by tutoring, making presentations that highlight their areas of expertise, and working alongside young friends in community service projects. Likewise, elementary students can venture beyond the classroom by establishing ongoing relationships

LEARNING THROUGH LITERATURE: CHILDREN'S BOOKS THAT CONFRONT AGEIST STEREOTYPES

Arkin, A. (1995). *Some fine grandpa!* New York: HarperCollins. Grandpa has some wild stories to tell when he comes to live with Molly and her family. Can they possibly be true? This humorous picture book raises subtle questions about the assumptions that often surround seniors.

Babbitt, N. (1975). *Tuck everlasting.* New York: Farrar, Straus & Giroux. In this classic, Newbery award-winning book, the protagonists partake of a fountain of youth and face the prospect and horror of not ever experiencing the aging process.

Bauer, M. D. (1995). *When I go camping with Grandma.* New York: Bridgewater. In this multi-generational celebration of life in the great outdoors, Grandma is portrayed as active, capable, and competent.

Bawden, N. (1996). *Granny the pag.* New York: Clarion. This young adult novel features an older protagonist, who shatters the stereotype of the typical elderly woman. The grandmother is a bit rough and eccentric, while at the same time gentle and nurturing. When her granddaughter's well-being is at stake, Granny rises to the occasion and demonstrates grace, dignity, and wisdom in the face of adversity.

Bunting, E. (1989). *The Wednesday surprise.* New York: Clarion. In this lovely intergenerational story, Anna and her grandmother work together on a special birthday project. The book demonstrates the power of a reciprocal relationship between young and old, one in which all participants contribute and benefit.

Bunting, E. (1994). *Sunshine home.* New York: Clarion. In this beautifully crafted picture book, three generations deal with a grandmother's entrance into a nursing home. Bunting's moving text explores the complexities and challenges sometimes experienced by older adults and their families.

Gaffney, T. (1996). *Grandpa takes me to the moon.* Illustrated by Barry Root. New York: Tambourine. A former astronaut recounts, for his young grandson, his memories of going to the moon. Both an informational text and gentle bedtime story, this book honors the wealth of experience to which older adults can lay claim.

Lowry, L. (1993). *The giver.* Boston: Houghton Mifflin. This haunting young adult novel depicts life in a futuristic world. It poses questions about the treatment of the elderly and others who may not appear "useful" to modern society.

Say, A. (1995). *Stranger in the mirror.* Boston: Houghton Mifflin. Sam goes to bed a happy little boy, but awakes to find that he has aged into an old man. Although he looks old on the outside, he recognizes that he is still the same youthful person on the inside. Will others recognize this truth too? This provocative text challenges many age-related biases and assumptions.

Shaw, E. (1996). *Grandmother's alphabet.* Duluth, MN: Pfeifer-Hamilton. This inspiring concept book shows that grandmothers should not be stereotyped, but that they can live out any number of fascinating roles.

Strangis, J. (1993). *Grandfather's rock.* Boston: Houghton Mifflin. Told in the style of a traditional folktale, this story reminds readers that each one of us will one day be old. The author invites readers to consider society's treatment of older members in light of the golden rule (i.e., to treat the elderly how we ourselves would like to be treated as we age).

Yolen, J. (1997). *Miz Berlin walks.* New York: Philomel. This tender, yet powerful, picture book describes a very special intergenerational friendship, and shows the impact this type of relationship can have over the course of a lifetime.

Figure 1

with seniors. This can be done by way of pen pal or key pal (E-mail) relationships, or by establishing face-to-face friendships with older adults at local senior citizen centers or care facilities. This personal contact between young and old has the potential to benefit both groups by debunking stereotypes, nurturing intergenerational relationships, and facilitating participation in mutually beneficial relationships (Dallman & Power, 1997; Frego, 1995; Smith & Newman, 1993).

Students who participate in these types of activities will gain firsthand experience in interacting with older adults who have varied backgrounds, abilities, and interests. They also stand to develop more accurate and less biased perceptions about the nature of the aging process, as well

as a better understanding of the complexities associated with being older. To aid students and older participants in forging these relationships, teachers must help facilitate a positive, nurturing, and educational learning experience by clearly communicating the goals of the project, developing a realistic set of expectations for all participants, connecting the experience with other curricular areas, and providing ongoing support throughout the experience.

Between the Pages

Literature provides a wonderful means for exploring notions related to age. As children read about older characters, they have an opportunity to "meet" a host of seniors and to

---

MAKING THE CONNECTION:
INTERNET RESOURCES THAT ADDRESS AGE-RELATED ISSUES

U.S. Census Bureau:
www.census.gov/
This Web site provides a host of information related to many aspects of American society. It also includes current demographic information related to older adults.

Intergenerational Connections:
www.cyfernet.org/parent/inter.html
This site includes information for those interested in community-based intergenerational programs. The links provide access to a wealth of intergenerational resources including children's books, articles, position statements, videos, and study programs.

Generations Together:
www.gt.pitt.edu
These are the home pages of an international center for intergenerational studies, housed at the University of Pittsburgh. The site includes a solid overview of intergenerational programming, as well as some very helpful resources.

The Gerontological Society of America:
www.geron.org
This site has access to background information related to the study of aging and to the Gerontological Society.

Elderhostel Intergenerational:
www.elderhostel.org
These pages describe a variety of opportunities for older adults to partner with young relatives and friends, as part of the Elderhostel program, including hands-on activities, class work, and field trips.

United Generations Ontario:
www.intergenugo.org
In addition to program information, this site provides very helpful background information about intergenerational programming. There are many excellent resources here for both students and seniors.

American Association of Retired Persons (AARP):
www.aarp.org
AARP, the largest association for people over 50 in the U.S., offers links to a variety of senior advocacy information.

Figure 2

examine the workings of intergenerational relationships (see Figure 1). Unfortunately, research indicates that a significant amount of age-related bias exists in the pages of children's books, often in the form of underrepresentation of older adults (Ansello, 1978). Moreover, when older characters *are* present, they often are depicted as sedentary people who have few outside interests; these characters are represented, both visually and textually, in very stereotypical roles, wearing only traditional clothing and rarely engaging in activities beyond those associated with grandparenting (Ansello, 1978; Crawford, 1996; McElhoe, 1999; McGuire, 1993). Therefore, it is essential that teachers take care when choosing books for read alouds and classroom use, striving to provide broadly representative examples of older adults.

Teachers also may wish to use children's books as points of cultural critique—springboards from which children can examine representations of older people in text. Even young children can be encouraged to ask thoughtful questions about the ways that certain groups are represented in books, and to explore the ways in which these representations both come from and support prevailing societal attitudes. Thus, even texts that are stereotypical, or that include negative representations of seniors, can be useful—as a means of exploring the basis of bias and to teach important concepts related to ageism.

Flipping the Flop

Was the teacher's lesson described at the beginning of this article really a flop? If so, did it have to be? More than likely, the children's responses to *Love You Forever* were symptomatic of their limited understanding of the very complex issues contained within the pages of the text. Understanding the ongoing cycle of human growth and development, the challenges of aging, and the joy of nurturing loving intergenerational relationships requires a degree of maturity and sophistication. Thus, it is not surprising that the children were not immediately as empathic as the teacher expected them to be. On the other hand, the children's lack of response also represented a window of opportu-

nity, one through which the teacher might glimpse her students' current understandings and then make plans accordingly to help them extend their learning, interact with sensitive texts in more appropriate ways, and ultimately develop accurate, positive, and healthy concepts about the aging process. In short, a negative response from the students is more of an opportunity for instruction than an obstacle to learning; it is a directive that helps point the way to areas in which the children would benefit from extended learning and new experiences related to these sensitive and important topics. As teachers, we can help students deal with important life lessons, and to flip "flop" lessons into powerful learning experiences.

References

Ansello, E. F. (1978). Ageism—The subtle stereotype. *Childhood Education, 54,* 118-122.

Blunk, E. M., & Williams, S. W. (1997). The effects of curriculum on preschool children's perceptions of the elderly. *Educational Gerontology, 23,* 233-241.

Carter, J. (1998). *The virtues of aging.* New York: Ballantine.

Comfort, A. (1976). *A good age.* New York: Crown.

Crawford, P. (1996). "Grandma: What gray hair you have!" Confronting ageism in the pages of children's literature. *Teaching and Learning Literature, 6,* 2-9.

Dallman, M. E., & Power, S. A. (1997). Forever friends: An intergenerational program. *Young Children, 52,* 64-68.

Derman-Sparks, L., & the ABC Task Force. (1989). *Anti-bias curriculum: Tools for empowering young children.* Washington, DC: National Association for the Education of Young Children.

Frego, R. J. (1995). Uniting the generations with music programs. *Music Educators Journal, 6,* 17-19, 55.

McElhoe, J. S. (1999). Images of grandparents in children's literature. *New Advocate, 12,* 249-258.

McGuire, S. L. (1993). Promoting positive attitudes toward aging: Literature for young children. *Childhood Education, 69,* 204-210.

Munsch, R. (1986). *Love you forever.* Willowdale, ON: Firefly.

Pipher, M. (1999). *Another country: Navigating the emotional terrain of our elders.* New York: Penguin.

Seefeldt, C., Warman, B., Jantz, R. K., & Galper, A. (1990). *Young and old together.* Washington, DC: National Association for the Education of Young Children.

Smith, T. B., & Newman, S. (1993). Older adults in early childhood programs: Why and how. *Young Children, 48,* 32-35.

U.S. Census Bureau. (1999). U.S. Census Bureau: United States Department of Commerce. [On-line]. Available: www.census.gov/

Classroom Configurations

Chapter 4
Finally, Heterogeneous Learning

Kathleen Glascott Burriss,
Middle Tennessee State University

The reauthorization in 1997 of the Individuals With Disabilities Education Act (U.S. Department of Education, 1997) mandates access to public schools for children with disabilities, but regular educators question the act's effectiveness. This chapter discusses the concerns of regular educators and provides support for genuine heterogeneous learning communities (Villa, Jacqueline, Meyers, & Nevin, 1996).

Introduction
Several professional organizations have issued position statements to support inclusion (see Figure 1) (Vaughn, Schumm, Jallad, Slusher, & Saumell, 1996). Classroom teachers, however, may still express discomfort about the practice. Despite public law or school district policy, it will be the general educator, as primary service-deliverer, who will ultimately interpret and implement programs. In other words, regardless of the goals set forth by a student's Individual Education Plan (IEP), it will be the classroom teacher's attitude that determines the success of inclusion programs.

Difficulties
According to Vaughn et al. (1996), teachers most frequently say class size has the most influence on the inclusion process. Resources (in particular, additional personnel) also are identified as contributing to effective inclusion. In addition, teachers believe administrators need to be aware of classroom concerns when establishing inclusion programs (Vaughn et al., 1996). School districts

that say they support inclusion may not provide adequate facilities and personnel to ensure integrated settings.

Finally, teachers are rightly concerned about overall funding, and how it may affect their accountability (Vaughn et al., 1996). Because of inclusion, special education classes may not exist. Therefore, students with disabilities may not be receiving needed services (Voyles, 1996).

Wood (1998) suggests that each new role demanded by inclusion programs causes additional stress on both regular and special educators. Classroom teachers express concern that their philosophical orientation, instructional considerations, and personalities may differ from those of special educators. Collaboration between special and general educators, however, may provide an effective inclusion model (Vaughn et al., 1996). Successful inclusion will require the combined efforts of regular and special education teachers (Graden & Bauer, 1992; Hanson & Widerstrom, 1993; Pugach, 1995).

Benefits
Through inclusion, children with disabilities are able to not only increase their academic learning, but also develop social skills (Voyles, 1996). Regardless of earned diplomas or special training, students with disabilities need to be competent in communication, negotiation, and cooperation with their nondisabled peers. Social skills training is best rehearsed in a natural setting—the classroom.

It is not only the disabled students who profit from inclusion, but also the typical student. If you

33

believe the world is heterogeneous, that is, composed of different people, then inclusionary settings make perfect human sense. Expect, accept, accommodate: If we expect difference, our disposition to accept is enhanced, and thereby our ability to accommodate will be heightened (Arizona State University, 1995).

Nondisabled students benefit through real-life interactions with their peers with disabilities. Through conversation, play, and shared projects, their ability to empathize and communicate is enhanced. Unfortunately, while general educators most frequently identify communication among teachers and the use of cooperative learning as necessary for successful inclusion, many remain doubtful about the effects of placing students with and without disabilities together (Vaughn et al., 1996). Teachers' perceptions regarding their roles

and their expectations of learners remain critical to inclusion outcomes. Ideally, educators implementing developmentally appropriate practice will design IEPs for learners both with and without disabilities. Evaluation is on a continuum. Students with disabilities do learn. For some, whether or not student learning is deemed "enough" remains an issue. Advantages to inclusion may lie in how we define schools and learning.

Partnership

According to Villa and Thousand (1992), a collaborative teaching model allows regular and special educators to merge their unique skills, foster feelings of positive interdependence, develop creative problem-solving skills, and share accountability. A partnership model may lessen general educators' concerns. Classroom teachers are

---

POSITION STATEMENTS IN SUPPORT OF INCLUSION

American Federation of Teachers. (1993). *Draft AFT position on inclusion.* (Available from the American Federation of Teachers, 555 New Jersey Avenue, NW, Washington, DC 20001.)

Association for Persons With Severe Handicaps. (1991). *The Association for Persons With Severe Handicaps resolutions and policy statement.* (Available from The Association for Persons With Severe Handicaps, 11201 Greenwood Avenue, N., Seattle, WA 98133.)

Council for Exceptional Children. (1993). *CEC policy on inclusive schools and community settings.* (Available from the Council for Exceptional Children, 1920 Association Drive, Reston, VA 22091-9494.)

Council for Learning Disabilities. (1993). Concerns about the "full inclusion" of students with learning disabilities in regular education classrooms. *Learning Disabilities Quarterly, 16*, 126.

Division for Learning Disabilities. (1993). *Inclusion: What does it mean for students with learning disabilities?* (Available from the Division for Learning Disabilities of the Council for Exceptional Children, 1920 Association Drive, Reston, VA 22091-9494.)

Learning Disabilities Association. (1993). *Position paper on full inclusion of all students with learning disabilities in the regular education classroom.* (Available from the Learning Disabilities Association, 4156 Library Road, Pittsburgh, PA 15234.)

National Association of State Boards of Education. (1992). *Winners all: From mainstreaming to inclusion.* (Available from the National Association of State Boards of Education, 1012 Cameron Street, Alexandria, VA 22314.)

National Education Association. (1989). *Resolution B-20: Education for all students with disabilities.* (Available from the National Education Association, 1201 16th Street, NW, Washington, DC 20036.)

National Joint Committee on Learning Disabilities. (1993). Providing appropriate education for students with learning disabilities in regular education classrooms. *Journal of Learning Disabilities, 26,* 330-332.

Taken from Vaughn, S., Schumm, J. S., Jallad, B., Slusher, J., & Saumell, L. (1996). Teachers' views of inclusion. *Learning Disabilities Research & Practice, 11*(2), 96-106.

Figure 1

worried they are not trained in the skills necessary to mediate special populations. Partnerships may use and expand teachers' skills in different ways; teachers may come to perceive their weaknesses as strengths. Collaboration presumes teachers believe all children can learn and assumes that, as educators, they have something to contribute to this learning process.

By definition, collaborative efforts imply a sharing of expectations, responsibilities, and effort. Children's progress should be a shared issue of professional pride, not an issue of turf. When general and special educators do not communicate, the child will lose. Neither the special nor the classroom teacher possess all the knowledge and strategies essential to mediate a single child's progress. Only when both disciplines appreciate the child as a whole is inclusion effective.

Voices in Partnership

Wood (1998) recommends the education partners' responsibilities be clearly articulated. Both regular and special education teachers need to be made aware of their partners' assumptions, practices, and terminology. Teachers who have had successful experiences need to share knowledge. In other words, teachers need to talk to one another.

Belonging is an important consideration. If teachers do not believe that children with disabilities belong in the school community, the students will not be included, regardless of legal mandates. Inclusion does not ensure "includedness."

Inclusion is complex and involves parents, regular and special educators, administrators, and politicians. However, the final word belongs to the children with special needs themselves, and the ultimate responsibility for this implementation resides with public educators. In an attempt to establish effective inclusive practices, identifying a few easy strategies to accommodate diverse learners is inappropriate. The variety of disabilities and the broad range within each disability group are too great to generalize a few strategies. To haphazardly implement strategies without thinking through an inclusion program may seriously diminish the ability of participants to succeed. This is why special and regular educators must work

together, pooling their strengths and compensating for one another's weaknesses. The special educator has the knowledge base regarding the disability and focuses on specificity. In contrast, the regular educator understands the curriculum and perceives the child as an individual as well as a member of the classroom. In this way, the regular educator serves to maintain curriculum and social balance for children with special needs while mediating for disabilities.

In moving toward a partnership on behalf of children with special needs, the following prompts may prove helpful for both regular and special educators.

• *Check your attitudes towards children with special needs and, in general, reconsider your notion of inclusion in public education.* Regular educators' lack of knowledge in the field of special education is a reality. However, it is not an excuse for declining to engage with children with disabilities. It is impossible for teacher education courses to prepare teachers for all varieties and ranges of disabilities. This is why the partnership with special educators is vital. Effective inclusion depends on participants' attitudes toward children with disabilities and the role of inclusion in public education.

• *Be knowledgeable regarding the child.* In addition to knowing about the child's disability, be familiar with the child both as an individual and as a participant in the learning community as a whole. Because regular and special education fields are distinct, the focus educators bring to each child is different. In collaboration, by joining special and regular educators' expertise, a rich and whole picture of each child can be developed. While it is important to understand the disability, the child's identity as a person should not be confused with the disability itself. Strive to build on the child's positive aspects.

• *Consider the family context.* As is true with all children, the family's perceptions of the child's abilities are crucial. Perception is reality. When educators are aware of family members' expectations for the child, and are familiar with the child's role when interacting within the family, they are better able to plan and implement an effective Individual Education Plan. The family is a material resource; more important, the family extends the emotional support essential to maintaining effective inclusive attitudes.

• *Technology is a useful tool.* Technology does not replace the human interaction between teacher and child. Technology is a way to access, organize, and present information. The child's self concept should be established apart from the performance made possible through the technology. The human relationship established between the child and the teacher remains the primary instructional factor. Significant gains in assistive technology have been made. However, the tools hold only as much potential as the user chooses.

In order to extend educators' understanding of inclusive practices, the following list provides suggested reading:

ADPRIMA-Toward the Best Education Information Choices. Retrieved April 30, 2002, from www.adprima.com/mainmenu.htm

Bartlett, L. D., Weisenstein, G. R., & Etscheidt, S. (2002). *Successful inclusion for educational leaders.* Upper Saddle River, NJ: Merrill/Prentice Hall.

Choate, J. S. (Ed.). (2000). *Successful inclusive teaching: Proven ways to detect and correct special needs* (3rd ed.). Boston: Allyn & Bacon.

Inclusion—Children who learn together, learn to live together. Retrieved April 30, 2002, from www.uni.edu/coe/inclusion

Intervention Central. Retrieved April 30, 2002, from www.interventioncentral.org

Kame'enui, E. J., Carnine, D. W., Dixon, R. C., Simmons, D. C., & Coyne, M. D. (2002). *Effective teaching strategies that accommodate diverse learners* (2nd ed.). Upper Saddle River, NJ: Merrill/Prentice Hall.

Kochhar, C. A., West, L. L., & Taymans, J. M. (2000). *Successful inclusion: Practical strategies for a shared responsibility.* Upper Saddle River, NJ: Merrill/Prentice Hall.

L.D. Online. Retrieved April 30, 2002, from www.ldonline.org

Mastropieri, M. A., & Scruggs, T. E. (2000). *The inclusive classroom: Strategies for effective instruction.* Upper Saddle River, NJ: Merrill/Prentice Hall.

Polloway, E. A., Patton, J. R., & Serna, L. (2001). *Strategies for teaching learners with special needs* (7th ed.).

Upper Saddle River, NJ: Merrill/Prentice Hall.

Salend, S. J. (2001). *Creating inclusive classrooms: Effective and reflective practices* (4th ed.). Upper Saddle River, NJ: Merrill/Prentice Hall.

Conclusion

Schooling should be more than mere academics. Public education also should instill and nurture character, democracy, and social consciousness. This is best achieved in a heterogeneous school. It is undeniably difficult for special and regular educators to overcome these issues in order to achieve meaningful partnerships on behalf of children with special needs. However, what is the alternative? Some professionals continue to argue that the inclusion model does not belong in public schools. Yet, the federal government ensures that public school education will represent and serve all students. Children with disabilities are real people. Therefore, receiving instruction in the least restrictive environment is their constitutional right. The challenges wrought by inclusion are worthy goals if one considers the social, political, and moral ramifications if inclusive practices are negated.

General and special educators are equal partners in the education of all children. Decision-making should be expanded to include teachers, students, and community (Villa, Jacqueline, Meyers, & Nevin, 1996). When the school community takes ownership of the inclusion process, intervention will happen more naturally. When partnerships between special and general educators are realized, then truly heterogeneous learning for all children occurs.

References

Arizona State University. (1995). Early childhood conference theme. Tempe, AZ: Author.

Graden, J. L., & Bauer, A. M. (1992). Using a collaborative approach to support students and teachers in inclusive classrooms. In S. Stainback & W. Stainback (Eds.), *Curriculum considerations in inclusive classrooms: Facilitating learning for all students* (pp. 85-100). Baltimore: Paul H. Brookes.

Hanson, M. J., & Widerstrom, A. H. (1993). Consultation and collaboration: Essentials of integration efforts for young children. In C. A. Peck, S. L. Odom, & D. D. Bricker (Eds.), *Integrating young children with disabilities into community programs: Ecological*

perspectives on research implementation (pp. 149-168).
Baltimore: Paul H. Brookes.

Pugach, M. C. (1995). On the failure of imagination in
inclusive schooling. *Journal of Special Education, 29,*
212-223.

U.S. Department of Education. (1997). 34 CFR Parts
300, 301, and 303. Assistance to states for the
education of children with disabilities, preschool
grants for children with disabilities, and early
intervention program for infants and toddlers with
disabilities; proposed rule. *Federal Register, 62*(204).

Vaughn, S., Schumm, J. S., Jallad, B., Slusher, J., &
Saumell, L. (1996). Teachers' views of inclusion.
Learning Disabilities Research & Practice, 11(2), 96-106.

Villa, R. A., Jacqueline, S. T., Meyers, H., & Nevin, A.
(1996). Teacher and administrator perceptions of
heterogeneous education. *Exceptional Children, 63*(1),
29-45.

Villa, R. A., & Thousand, J. S. (1992). Student collabo-
ration: An essential for curriculum delivery in the
21st century. In S. Stainback & W. Stainback (Eds.),
*Curriculum considerations in inclusive classrooms:
Facilitating learning for all students* (pp. 117-142).
Baltimore: Paul H. Brookes.

Voyles, L. C. (1996). Inclusion—Where we are today?
CEC Today, 3(3).

Wood, M. (1998). Whose job is it anyway? Educational
roles in inclusion. *Exceptional Children, 64*(2), 181-195.

Chapter 5
Defining the Multiage Classroom

Sandra J. Stone,
Northern Arizona University

Many schools throughout the United States are beginning to use multiage classrooms. Multiage educators are finding, however, that while some schools purport to be establishing multiage classrooms, they are not really doing so. Often, a mixed-age grouping is the only defining part of such a classroom, with the rest of the multiage philosophy left out of the design. These classrooms are merely "combination" classrooms, resembling classrooms of the past rather than the multiage classroom of today. Usually, these combination classes are the result of a school not having enough children to fill two grade levels. Unfortunately, the term "multiage" is frequently tagged onto these combination classes because it is the new fashion in education terminology. Yet, it is very important to distinguish between the combination class and the multiage class, because they embrace two different education philosophies.

Typically, the two grades are taught separately in the combination classroom. In a 1st- and 2nd-grade combination class, for example, the 1st-graders and 2nd-graders have separate prescribed curricula. The teacher tries to provide for the two groups in the best way possible. He meets with the 1st-graders, teaching them their reading or math concepts, and then does the same with the 2nd-graders. It is a difficult set-up, but somewhat manageable.

The mixed-age grouping, by definition, is created deliberately for the *benefit* of the children, not as a way to balance class sizes. A simple definition of the multiage classroom is a mixed-age group of children who stay with the same teacher for several years. Such a group is formed to "optimize what can be learned when children of different—as well

as the same—ages and abilities have opportunities to interact" (Katz, Evangelou, & Hartman, 1990, p. 1). Multiage classrooms often have an age span of three years rather than two, providing greater opportunities for cross-age learning (Stone & Christie, 1996).

Learning is structured over several years with the same teacher, so that the children can enjoy continuous progress and success. The teacher is able to see children as individuals progressing on their own continuum of learning, and to use appropriate instructional strategies and assessments to accommodate each child's needs.

Retention and promotion are not components of multiage classrooms, because their designers view learning as a developmental process. Teachers use process teaching strategies rather than a prescribed curriculum. Multiage teachers know that a prescribed curriculum usually does not meet the needs of all the children. With no grade-level expectations, each child is individually supported to make successful progress on his own continuum of learning. Learning opportunities are challenging, but appropriate.

Instruction is not separated by age or grade; rather, children become a family of learners who benefit from collaboration. Mixed-age classrooms provide natural social learning environments that support rich cross-age learning. Cognitively, both younger and older children benefit from having to resolve conflicting points of view. Younger children gain new understandings and older children solidify their mastery of skills (Brown & Palincsar, 1986; Roopnarine & Johnson, 1984; Trudge & Caruso, 1988). The age differences also lead mixed-age children to engage in more prosocial behaviors, such as helping, sharing, and taking turns (Katz, Evangelou, & Hartman, 1990).

In looking at the multiage classroom's environment, curriculum, and assessment, one can see that its structure is based on what we know about children and how they learn. First, the environment is carefully planned in order to take advantage of experiential and mixed-age learning opportunities. Learning tables and centers are used instead of individual desks. Centers are designed to be open-ended, so that all children can come into the experiences at their own level of understanding and skill. The centers allow children choice and opportunities for both autonomous and cooperative learning (Stone, 1996).

Second, the multiage curriculum reflects a child-centered, rather than a curriculum-centered, approach. It is a common misconception that multiage teachers choose a middle-of-the-road curriculum in order to manage the curriculum. It would be inappropriate, however, for a multiage teacher of grades 1, 2, and 3 to choose a 2nd-grade curriculum. Parents would worry, and rightly so, that older children would not be challenged enough and that the younger children would be frustrated by material that is too difficult. In a true multiage classroom, the teacher presents appropriate skills within the meaningful context of process learning. Children learn to read as they read, write as they write, and problem solve as they solve real problems. Each child enters the process at precisely his or her own learning rate and level. In addition, multiage teachers open up the curriculum for *all* children, exposing them to much more material than they would enjoy in a same-grade classroom. As Brouchard (1991) notes, children "can 'plug into' the curriculum at the appropriate level and yet be exposed to opportunities for review as well as for acceleration" (p. 30).

The teacher uses whole group strategies, such as shared reading, modeled writing, writers' workshops, and discovery science. He or she also uses small-group strategies, such as guided math or reading based on the needs of the children, not on their age or grade. In addition, the children learn from each other by working at centers or on projects.

Assessment in the multiage classroom is also conducted deliberately for the children's benefit. Graded report cards that label, rank, and sort children are not necessary. Instead, multiage teachers use portfolios. Such authentic assessment allows multiage teachers to document each child's growth and development within the process and contexts of their actual learning. The knowledge the teacher gains from the assessments is then used to guide and support appropriate instruction for the child. Children are evaluated on their own achievements and potential (Anderson & Pavan, 1993), rather than in comparison to norms or grade-level expectations. Each child in the multiage setting is able to enjoy success through portfolio assessment.

We often find that combination classes are created simply to manage children's behavior in order to accommodate uneven numbers of children among different grades, and to get the children through the graded curriculum. The true multiage classroom takes down the barriers of "gradedness" and seeks something different—it seeks to truly benefit children by fitting the school to their needs, instead of trying to fit the children to the school.

References

Anderson, R. H., & Pavan, B. N. (1993). *Nongradedness: Helping it to happen.* Lancaster, PA: Technomic Publishing.

Brouchard, L. (1991). Mixed grouping for gifted students. *The Gifted Child Today, 14*(76), 30-35.

Brown, A. L., & Palincsar, A. (1986). *Guided, cooperative learning and individual knowledge acquisition* (Technical Report No. 372). Champaign, IL: Center for the Study of Reading.

Katz, L., Evangelou, D., & Hartman, J. (1990). *The case for mixed-age grouping in early education.* Washington, DC: National Association for the Education of Young Children.

Roopnarine, J., & Johnson, J. (1984). Socialization in a mixed-age experimental program. *Developmental Psychology, 20*(5), 828-832.

Stone, S. J. (1996). *Creating the multiage classroom.* Glenview, IL: GoodYear Books.

Stone, S. J., & Christie, J. F. (1996). Collaborative literacy learning during sociodramatic play in a multiage (K-2) primary classroom. *Journal of Research in Childhood Education, 10*(2), 123-133.

Trudge, J., & Caruso, D. (1988). Cooperative problem solving in the classroom: Enhancing young children's cognitive development. *Young Children, 44*(1), 46-52.

Chapter 6
Bridging the Gap With Cross-Age Grouping

Patricia A. Crawford,
University of Central Florida

"They're big—really big!"
"They're mean."
"My sister's a big kid, but she's not mean."
"You have to stay out of their way— they could run you over."
"Big kids are so cool."

These are typical responses offered by 1st-graders who were asked to comment on their perceptions of the older children in their school community. Their responses reveal a mixture of fear, admiration, and awe. These children regard older students as a group set apart; a group that can be a bit intimidating, and with whom it is best to have guarded contacts.

These perceptions are not surprising. Modern elementary schools typically have been structured as age-segregated cultures, allowing few opportunities for the oldest and youngest students to interact meaningfully. Grade levels are separated, and the distinction between primary and intermediate students often is sharp and extends to all areas of the school day. Typically, children not only are segregated into homogeneous age groups for academic work, but also are often clustered by age groups for lunch, recess, and extracurricular activities. This type of segregation leaves students with few opportunities for social interaction across age groups, and can prevent a school community's diverse members from building cohesion and a sense of connection.

Bridging the Gap

Given these issues, it seems only reasonable that many educators are seeking to restructure school programs in ways that facilitate interaction among children of varying age levels. These restructuring efforts are meant to create inclusive school communities in which age and experience differences are considered to be assets, rather than liabilities (Katz, Evangelou, & Hartman, 1990).

Many schools have addressed the gap between children of varying age and experience levels by restructuring their classrooms into multiage communities (Stone, 1996). Multiage programs can provide wonderful opportunities for interaction among students at adjacent, or clustered, grade levels (Chase & Doan, 1994, 1996). Multiage programs also tend to be fully developed and comprehensive, affecting nearly every aspect of the children's school day. Successful implementation requires the support of all involved parties, including teachers, administrators, students, and parents.

Cross-age grouping differs from multiage

41

grouping in several ways. While multiage classrooms bring together children who are relatively close in age, cross-age programs are designed to bring together children whose ages differ by more than one year, and, in many cases, whose ages reflect opposite ends of the school spectrum. Cross-age programs also differ from multiage programs in terms of scope and implementation. Unlike multiage programs, which affect nearly every aspect of the curriculum and school day, cross-age programs tend to be less comprehensive. In cross-age programs, older and younger children typically maintain their own classrooms, but are brought together at certain times of the day to work as a cohesive whole.

Cross-age experiences can take a number of different forms, ranging from a highly structured academic tutoring program to a collaborative community project, to simply providing the opportunity for children to develop informal, healthy relationships with students of different ages and experience levels. Cross-age experiences can be either short- or long-term and can involve some or all members of the school community. Because of the flexibility inherent in these programs, many teachers find cross-age grouping to be a workable and effective alternative to the age-segregated structure that characterizes most elementary schools. Smaller cross-age projects are a good starting place for teachers who wish to develop a multiage program, but who do not yet have the necessary support from parents, administrators, or other school personnel.

Looking Back at Cross-Age Grouping

Although it is often innovatively implemented, cross-age grouping is not a new concept. Learning experiences in which older and younger children join together to engage in social and educational partnerships have been likened to the relationships that exist among family members (Rekrut, 1994). In this very natural context, parents, extended family members, and older siblings all share in the joys, as well as the responsibilities, of nurturing younger family members. Older family members share their expertise and serve as natural initiators, compassionate caregivers, and thought-ful teachers. Younger family members learn and grow within a supportive context and also have opportunities to make significant contributions to this most natural of relationships. Similarly, cross-age programs offer opportunities for older and younger community members to interact in authentic ways, to participate in a helping relationship, and to engage in meaningful learning.

Beyond the scope of home and family learning, cross-age educational experiences also have a strong historical precedent within the world of schooling. In 19th-century England, Joseph Lancaster established the monitorial system of instruction. Believing that children learn best when they have the opportunity to learn from one another, Lancaster developed a tutorial system in which older students were responsible for teaching and monitoring the progress of younger students (Fogarty & Wang, 1982; Gutek, 1972 as cited in Rekrut, 1994).

In 18th- and 19th-century America, the one-room schoolhouse provided an environment in which children of all ages learned together, in the same room, and under the supervision of the same teacher. The extent to which these teachers invoked a cross-age philosophy and facilitated partnerships between younger and older pupils, however, varied a great deal from region to region, and from school to school.

In the 1970s, cross-age grouping was revived and invoked as a means of addressing the issues of scant funding, limited resources, and teacher shortages (Rekrut, 1994). In these settings, cross-age grouping often was positioned as an extension of school-based peer-tutoring programs, and was viewed as a means through which teachers could individualize instruction and provide added support for at-risk students (Bean & Luke, 1972; Smith, 1988).

Today, cross-age connections take many different forms—including book buddies, writing partners, tutors, and collaborative innovators—allowing children of different ages to work together towards many different goals and in a host of different settings (Caserta-Henry, 1996; Fulton, LeRoy, & Pinckney, 1994; Henriques, 1997; Leland & Fitzpatrick, 1993-94; Samway, Whang, & Pippitt, 1995).

CROSS-AGE EXPERIENCES

Getting Started

Book Buddies: Create a book buddies program in which students of different grade levels get together to read, discuss, and respond to literature. Both older and younger children can take turns reading picture books.

Pen Pals: Students at different grade levels can become pen pals, forging ongoing relationships that span age levels and using their writing skills in an authentic, purposeful way.

Writing Coaches: Invite older children to assist younger partners with their writing by recording dictations, conducting peer writing conferences, assisting with the editing process, and helping prepare for final publication.

Artists in Residence: Older students can act as "artists in residence" by modeling, facilitating, and nurturing a variety of artistic techniques among younger, less experienced students.

Moving On

Tutoring Pairs: Older students tutor younger children in an academic area. This arrangement provides one-on-one support for tutees, while older students gain additional reinforcement of skills, content, and learning processes.

Social Advocates: Invite students of different ages to address a community issue. Students can work together to share concerns, develop priorities, construct an action plan, and work together to make a difference.

Actor Guilds: Create a cross-age thespian group in which children of varying ages come together to engage in dramatic events and perform plays for the school community.

Play Partners: Encourage students to engage in cross-age play and social activities by arranging group games and activities. Older students can take leadership roles, or teach younger children how to play new games.

Why Bother?

Cross-age grouping's benefits are many and varied. They extend to both older and younger participants, as well as to teachers and other members of the school community. Numerous studies chronicling the academic progress made by participants in cross-age tutoring programs indicate that these programs benefit both tutors and tutees and that they result in academic gains. The structure of cross-age programs allows younger participants to receive personal attention, individualized instruction, and immediate responses to their questions and concerns (Fox & Wright, 1997; Henriques, 1997). By working with a more experienced student, they benefit from Vygotsky's (1978) zone of proximal development, in which they experience success working in collaboration with others, which eventually leads them to later success when working on their own.

Older participants also can experience academic benefits. As older students work with content material and determine ways to make this material interesting and accessible to the younger participants, they gain the opportunity to practice skills, explore different aspects of the subject, and use their knowledge in new ways. Essentially, they learn more effectively through having the opportunity to teach others (Nevi, 1983; Rekrut, 1994).

Carefully developed, ongoing cross-age pro-grams also have the potential to positively affect students' attitudes towards school, learning, and fellow members of the school community (Caserta-Henry, 1996; Fogarty & Wang, 1982; Raschke, Dedrick, Strathe, Yoder, & Kirkland, 1988; Schneider & Barone, 1997). Younger students benefit from receiving personalized atten-tion and from gaining the confidence that comes through working with older, respected members of the school. For older participants, much of the positive impact may spring from having the opportunity to contribute to and fully participate in a helping relationship. The very nature of a cross-age partnership makes it possible for older students of varied interests and abilities to be cast in the roles of nurturers, caregivers, and teachers.

Even students who have struggled in other academic and social settings can flourish when working with younger children, as they discover leadership potential that previously had gone untapped. As these students work with younger children, they also may develop a stronger sense of self-esteem, experience new insights about what it means to be both a teacher and a learner, and gain a deeper sense of the empathy that comes from working closely with others (Nevi, 1983; Schneider & Barone, 1997).

Quality Programs

Getting started on a cross-age collaboration is not difficult. It begins simply with the interest and commitment of two teachers who wish to forge a partnership between grade levels and who share a vision for the academic, social, and affective benefits that can result from such a collaboration. Although the experience may take a number of different forms, certain elements appear to be characteristic of successful programs. First, both faculty and administrators must be committed to the program's philosophy. This commitment is demonstrated through enthusiasm, preparation, and the allocation of necessary time and funding. Second, older students must receive adequate support to ensure their success within the framework of the collaboration. Student tutors, for example, could be taught practical strategies to help them identify quality instructional materials, plan lessons, and document progress. Third, there must be an element of student ownership. All students need to have the opportunity to give valuable input and make meaningful decisions concerning the nature, content, and processes of their learning. Finally, there must be ongoing program evaluation, with modifications made as deemed necessary (Raschke et al., 1988; Rekrut, 1994; Schneider & Barone, 1997).

Cross-age experiences provide wonderful opportunities for teaching and learning, as well as for building a sense of community among diverse members of the school population. In the words of the 1st-graders who participated in an ongoing literature partnership with 6th-grade students:

I loved it. The [cross-age] storybook project was the best part of the year.

I wish we could work with our [6th-grade] buddies every day!

A 6th-grader who participated in the same partnership wrote the following entry as her final reflection:

My favorite part of the year has been working with the 1st-graders. At first, I didn't know how our project would turn out, but in the end it was really great. I really liked being with the little kids, and I still talk to them all the time when I see them on the playground. I want to do more things like this. Maybe I'll be a teacher when I grow up.

Cross-age collaborations open a world of opportunities for all those involved. They should not be overlooked as a potential strategy for supporting instruction and nurturing growth.

References

Bean, R., & Luke, C. (1972). As a teacher I've been learning . . . *Journal of Reading, 16,* 128-132.

Caserta-Henry, C. (1996). Reading buddies: A first-grade intervention program. *The Reading Teacher, 49,* 500-503.

Chase, P., & Doan, J. (1994). *Full circle: A new look at multiage education.* Portsmouth, NH: Heinemann.

Chase, P., & Doan, J. (1996). *Choosing to learn: Ownership and responsibility in a primary multiage classroom.* Portsmouth, NH: Heinemann.

Fogarty, J. L., & Wang, M. C. (1982). An investigation of the cross-age peer tutoring process: Some implications for instructional design and motivation. *The Elementary School Journal, 82,* 451-469.

Fox, B. J., & Wright, M. (1997). Connecting school and home literacy experiences through cross-age reading. *The Reading Teacher, 50,* 396-403.

Fulton, L., LeRoy, C., & Pinckney, M. L. (1994). Peer education partners: A program for learning and working together. *TEACHING Exceptional Children, 26,* 6-8, 10-11.

Gutek, G. L. (1972). *A history of the western educational experience.* Prospect Heights, IL: Waveland.

Henriques, M. E. (1997). Increasing literacy among kindergartners through cross-age training. *Young Children, 52,* 42-47.

Katz, L., Evangelou, D., & Hartman, J. (1990). *The case for mixed-age grouping in early education.* Washington, DC: National Association for the Education of Young Children.

Leland, C., & Fitzpatrick, R. (1993-94). Cross-age interaction builds enthusiasm for reading and writing. *The Reading Teacher, 47,* 292-301.

Nevi, C. N. (1983). Cross-age tutoring: Why does it help the tutors? *The Reading Teacher, 47,* 292-301.

Raschke, D., Dedrick, C., Strathe, M., Yoder, M., & Kirkland, G. (1988). Cross-age tutorials and attitudes of kindergartners toward older students. *The Teacher Educator, 3,* 10-19.

Rekrut, M. D. (1994). Peer and cross-age tutoring: The lessons of research. *Journal of Reading, 37,* 356-362.

Samway, K. D., Whang, G., & Pippitt, M. (1995). *Buddy reading: Cross-age tutoring in a multicultural school.* Portsmouth, NH: Heinemann.

Schneider, R. B., & Barone, D. (1997). Cross-age tutoring. *Childhood Education, 73,* 136-143.

Smith, L. L. (1988). Cross-age tutoring—using the four t's. *Reading Horizons, 21,* 44-49.

Stone, S. J. (1996). *Creating the multiage classroom.* Glenview, IL: Good Year Books.

Vygotsky, L. (1978). *Mind in society: The development of higher psychological processes.* Cambridge, MA: Harvard University Press.

Reading Revisited

Chapter 7
Links to Literacy

Denise Dragich,
Indiana, Pennsylvania, Area School District

"Hey, teacher—look!
All those circle things and
hook things are the same!"

This excited comment came from David, one of the students in my first public school kindergarten class. David had watched and listened while I sang and pointed to the words of "The Hippopotamus Song," which were printed on chart paper. David's outburst taught me some things about him. First, he was listening and paying attention. Second, he was able to make observations, notice likenesses and differences, and make connections about symbols. It also taught me that David did not know that "those circle and hook things" were the letters "a" and "t" in the words "cat," "hat," and "bat." This interaction challenged the assumptions I held about David, his literacy learning, and my own teaching. I had to pause and consider what teaching approach would support David's literacy learning, as well as that of the other students.

Another event served to challenge my assumptions in a different way. During parent conferences, two different pairs of parents asked related questions. One pair asked, "Should we buy 'Hooked On Phonics' for our child?" The other pair asked, "Do you teach phonics in your classroom?" These parents were obviously concerned about their children's reading progress and wanted to support and ensure the children's

success. It seemed evident that they were hearing conflicting messages about the nature of effective reading instruction and wanted to make sure that they were proceeding in the best way possible. As a teacher, I had to be ready to articulate my personal philosophy and be able to help the parents understand the connection between our classroom practice and the theory that undergirds it. I had to assure them that, yes, I do teach phonics, but in a contextual fashion that might look different from their own memories of classroom learning. When asked what educational materials they should provide at home, I had to stress the importance of a broad and rich experience with language and texts, with phonics as only one small piece of that experience.

These two situations occurred at different times and in different classroom settings. However, they share a common thread: Methods of teaching reading continually come under question, by parents and teachers alike. As public and political venues influence the understanding of literacy learning, many groups become vocal about the best way to approach literacy instruction (Goodman, 1998; Shannon, 2000). Teachers are faced with ever-increasing demands to satisfy these audiences and the range of their students' needs. They are affected daily by the reality that many social, cultural, and political influences shape the practice of literacy learning (Shannon, 1992, 2001; Willis & Harris, 2000).

Since all teachers are affected by these influences and must make curricular decisions at some point, we must be keenly aware of our own stances on theoretical and practical beliefs. In addition to theory, we must have classroom evidence that supports our statements. Since teachers must make decisions about how best to proceed with literacy learning and teaching in their classrooms, it becomes the educator's challenge to enhance learning and literacy development for all students.

Thinking About Theory

Children learn language and literacy best when they use it and see it used in relevant and meaningful contexts in their lives (Smith, 1990). Like David, all students come to school knowing *something* and are able to make observations and connections. It is the teacher's role to build on students' knowledge and immerse them in purposeful and productive interactions with reading and print. At the same time, teachers are charged with satisfying the expectations of parents, administrators, and the increasingly dominant government-imposed educational standards. The question of "How do I proceed with literacy instruction?" is relevant in all these contexts and must be carefully addressed.

In traditional classrooms, literacy education has largely centered on reading of prescribed texts, fluency, comprehension, skill development, and more recently, writing. All of these factors are important in developing literate individuals, but the context and manner in which they are learned and taught are also very important. Reading is a social activity and children learn from the others with whom they interact. They first learn to read by having adults read to them and then move towards greater independence by having adults read with them (Fountas & Pinnell, 1996; Holdaway, 1979; Mooney, 1990). In these natural settings, children enter into joyful literacy transactions, reading to make sense of their world and to enjoy language and story. In keeping with this, literacy instruction should take place in a positive, affective, and social climate (Smith, 1998).

The Importance of Language Experiences

Au, Carroll, and Scheu (1997) tell us that many aspects are integral to a comprehensive and balanced literacy program. When teachers choose engaging and quality literature to share with children, they are also providing a variety of important instructional foundations. They are helping children to:

- Develop listening and comprehension skills
- Build a rich vocabulary base
- Become familiar with the pleasures of engaging language.

Sharing literature and giving children opportunities to participate in oral language activities in the form of songs and poetry allows literacy development and growth in a pleasurable, nonthreatening setting (Baskwill & Whitman, 1986). Teacher modeling and choral readings of these formats help children gain confidence in reading and see the connection between spoken words and print in an enjoyable and inviting context. The predictability and repetition of language that occurs in these formats not only build oral language skills, but also invite children to read and re-read (Jalongo & Ribblett, 1997).

Eric Carle's (1993) picture songbook *Today Is Monday* is one of many books that help to expose children to the pleasures of language. Children can enjoy the beautifully rendered illustrations as they sing their way through the days of the week:

Today is Monday, today is Monday
Monday, string beans
All you hungry children
Come and eat it up.

Today is Tuesday, today is Tuesday
Tuesday, spaghetti
Monday, string beans
All you hungry children
Come and eat it up…

Teachers can use the text as a linguistic scaffold, helping children to build on the language by first brainstorming lists of favorite foods and then creating their own innovations on the textual pattern, as in the following:

Today is Tuesday, today is Tuesday
Tuesday, chicken nuggets
Monday, pizza
All you hungry children
Come and eat it up.

As children transact with the text and include their own lyrical suggestions in the framework of the song's format, they add a personal connection. This not only adds an element of enjoyment, but also helps them to internalize language structures and become more sophisticated meaning makers (Fountas & Pinnell, 1996; Holdaway, 1979).

Similarly, a companion poem, such as Hoberman's (1981) "Yellow Butter," can serve as a valuable tool for helping children to celebrate language and strengthen their skills:

Yellow butter, purple jelly, red jam, black bread,
Spread it thick. Say it quick.
Yellow butter, purple jelly, red jam, black bread,
Spread it thicker. Say it quicker.
Yellow butter, purple jelly, red jam, black bread,
Don't talk with your mouth full!

When children are asked, "What do you notice about this poem?" they quickly notice that words

---

CREATURES EVERYWHERE, MY DARLING!
Adapted by Room 25

Mealworms in the backpack,
Ooo, worms, ooo.

Liz in our classroom
And a plastic one, too.
   [A classroom pet lizard was named Liz and there was an
   orange, plastic lizard in its cage]

Snakes in the grass,
What'll we do?

Creatures everywhere, my darling!

Kangaroos on the trampoline,
Go back to the zoo.

Cheetahs in the basement,
What will we do?

Turkeys in the garden,
I'll cook you!
   ["Shoo, shoo, shoo" was an alternate verse for several children
   who objected to cooking a turkey.]

Creatures everywhere, my darling!

Figure 1

repeat. They will also notice, or can be helped to notice, the more intricate differences between the words "thick" and "thicker," "quick" and "quicker." Thus, with a mini-lesson or discussion, the class can address the intricacy of language and proceed toward fuller literacy development.

Children need spoken, written, and musical language to promote literacy and other development. Poetic language encourages recognition of the link between sound and symbols and the predictability of rhyme allows children to exercise memory and problem-solving skills. Children will become familiar with poetry and song, and their own conventions (Gable, 1999). The aesthetic qualities of these formats lead to interactive social exchanges that help to embed children in a culture of literacy learning.

A Culture of Learning

Establishing a culture of learning that centers on literacy and language leads children to establish themselves in that culture, too. For example, *Skip to My Lou* (Westcott, 1989) was the featured read aloud in a 1st-grade classroom during a literature unit that integrated a scientific study of flies. When Lynn's father sent mealworms from his pet shop to feed the classroom pets and they "accidentally" spilled out into Lynn's backpack, she and her friend Nathan had the words and rhythm of the song so ingrained in their minds that they entered the classroom singing, "Mealworms in my backpack, ooh, worms, ooh!" The teacher heard their refrain and saw it as an opportunity for a literary event. The entire class was invited to extend Lynn's and Nathan's words into a song (see Figure 1) that became part of a class-published book they called *Creatures Everywhere, My Darling!*

Learning to read should be viewed primarily as a scholarly and social activity, regardless of the age, ability, or background of the learner. The skills of reading not only should be taught in a cohesive fashion, but also should be ingrained in a rich scholarly and social setting. Thematically organized text sets can be helpful in this regard. For example, *Skip to My Lou, Old Black Fly* (Aylesworth, 1992), and *I Know an Old Lady Who Swallowed a Fly* (Taback, 1997) are examples of

humorous and fanciful texts that all feature the common fly. These texts all play on the pleasures of language and use captivating illustrations. Classroom activities that relate to these texts lead to additional scholarly learning through extension and integration of other topics. In this case, nonfiction texts about flies can be presented and made available for exploration. A supply of fly larvae in a container can provide a concrete observational experience as the children watch the larvae change into pupae and develop into flies. Children's listening comprehension will be strengthened as they hear more involved texts and see the process occur.

Teachers can support this process further by helping students to form flexible small groups based on their personal reading interests. For example, a small group of students in my class showed consistent interest in the topic of penguins. After exploring both fictional and informational books on the topic, two boys discovered the humorous story *Tacky the Penguin* (Lester, 1988). Sam and Jacob responded to this book by integrating their knowledge of penguins into a song:

Tacky the Happy Penguin
(to the tune of Rudolph, the Red-nosed Reindeer)

Tacky the happy penguin had a razor sharp beak
And if you ever saw him, you would even say, "It's sharp!"
All of the other penguins used to laugh and call him names,
They never let poor Tacky join in any penguin games.
Then one freezing Antarctica night, hunters came to hunt.
Tacky sang his silly songs and the hunters ran away.
Then all the penguins loved him as they shouted out with glee,
"Tacky the happy penguin, you'll go down in history!"
        —by Sam and Jacob, with help from Room 27

These links across fiction and nonfiction texts provide valuable learning experiences and serve as great motivators to read and learn more. The children's responses to these texts are indicative of their learning, and demonstrate their content knowledge as well as their ability to use language structures and make texts their own.

Literacy in Relevant Contexts

In order to become literate and proficient readers, children must learn the effective use of phonics, grammar, spelling, and other conventions (Strickland, 1994-95). These literacy skills can be taught in meaningful contexts. Many writing activities can serve as a means for teaching these skills. One such method, writing the daily news, introduces the rules of phonics and grammar through a personal and interactive exchange.

The daily news is a language arts activity that builds literacy and learning through group interaction and mutual experiences. The children work together daily, during a regularly scheduled large-group time, to contribute ideas for classroom news. The children offer items that are pertinent to the classroom while the teacher prints the items on large chart paper. This daily writing serves as a basis for instruction. The teacher chooses a phonetic or grammatical rule and invites one of the students to circle all the words that fit that rule. The rest of the class must identify the selected rule. The teacher may offer news items of her own, reflecting a rule that she wishes to teach or review.

Once this procedure has been modeled sufficiently and the children have become more familiar with the structure of written language, the teacher begins to make intentional errors that the students must identify and correct. For example, punctuation may be omitted or a misspelling that reflects a phonetic rule (c for k, f for ph) may be included. This helps children gain familiarity with language structure in an enjoyable and nonthreatening setting.

Words gain more relevance when used in this holistic and personal format. Present and past tense become meaningful when writing takes place at the beginning or end of the day. Math learning can be built into the news, as the children record the time and temperature. Children also learn how to disagree and reach consensus. The class must agree on which news items are appropriate to record and on the best wording.

In the primary grades, writing the news is a method of introducing the rules of phonics and the grammatical aspects of language within a context. This activity helps children learn the rules of language without losing its holistic structure. Children in the upper grades can extend the previously mentioned learning. Students may be assigned the role of editor and be responsible for typing and revising the news on the computer. When published, the daily news can become part of a class history book or sent home with students to read with their families.

In addition to learning language rules, other learning evolves during this activity. Because the news is based on their experiences, children make personal connections with the written word. The children learn a method of reporting information and begin to understand the concept of audience. Some information may be termed personal news that belongs in a private journal, while some is designated class news that will be published and available for everyone to read. This gives the learner a chance to experience views from different perspectives and see how information can be perceived differently (Whitin & Whitin, 1998).

The following vignette, recorded by an observer in my classroom who was following the O. J. Simpson trials, illustrates some of this learning (Pattnaik, 1996). The 2nd-graders were suggesting news items.

Michael: O. J. Simpson is getting married.
Teacher: I heard something about this on TV, but what I heard said it wasn't true. So, we're not sure. How can we write something when we're not sure?
Children: Say "probably."
Tanya: I heard he found a place where he's wanted.
Teacher: What do you mean by wanted? Remember, we have to make sure everyone understands what we write.

A discussion ensued in which the dual meaning of "wanted" in this situation was examined and the possibility for misunderstanding if this word was used was explored.

Tanya: I mean people like him and want him to live there.
Teacher: Let's find a word for this.
Ricky: "Welcome"!

The daily news serves as a valuable instructional tool that:

- Introduces the rules of phonics and technical aspects of language, in context
- Uses the children's experiences as the resource
- Gives students the opportunity to argue and reach consensus
- Allows children to connect language to their personal lives
- Shows a method of reporting information. (Pattnaik, 1996)

This group writing activity brings several opportunities for assessment. The teacher can note children who are able to follow and identify the selected rules. Language skills and oral reading abilities are easily observable. Print awareness and the ability to make connections about letters and sounds quickly become evident. The teacher can use this time to make individual and valuable anecdotal observations about children.

Concluding Thoughts

Political and societal demands on educators remain constant. Questions about best practice and theoretical issues continue. Teachers must engage in their own professional development and reflection to be prepared to answer these questions and to satisfy the learning needs of their students. They must develop curriculum that is based on the needs, interests, and experiences of their students and that satisfies scholarly growth and learning. Since the classroom is the place where theory meets practice, teachers must provide rich content and opportunities for authentic learning and literacy experiences (Zemelman, Daniels, & Hyde, 1998).

References

Au, K. H., Carroll, J. H., & Scheu, J. A. (1997). *Balanced literacy instruction: A teacher's resource book.* Norwood, MA: Christopher Gordon Publishers.

Aylesworth, J. (1992). *Old black fly.* New York: Henry Holt & Co.

Baskwill, J., & Whitman, P. (1986). *The whole language sourcebook.* Ontario, Canada: Scholastic Canada.

Carle, E. (1993). *Today is Monday.* New York: Scholastic.

Fountas, I. C., & Pinnell, G. S. (1996). *Guided reading: Good first teaching for all children.* Portsmouth, NH: Heinemann.

Gable, S. (1999). Promote children's literacy with poetry. *Young Children, 54*(5), 12-15.

Goodman, K. S. (Ed.). (1998). *In defense of good teaching: What teachers need to learn about the reading wars.* York, ME: Stenhouse Publications.

Hoberman, M. A. (1981). *Yellow butter, purple jelly, red jam, black bread.* New York: Viking Penguin.

Holdaway, D. (1979). *The foundations of literacy.* Portsmouth, NH: Heinemann.

Jalongo, M. R., & Ribblett, D. M. (1997). Using song picture books to support emergent literacy. *Childhood Education, 74,* 15-22.

Lester, H. (1988). *Tacky the penguin.* New York: Houghton Mifflin Co.

Mooney, M. (1990). *Reading to, with and by children.* Katonah, NY: Richard C. Owen.

Pattnaik, J. (1996). *A biographical study of the reflective practices of aspiring and practicing early childhood practitioners.* Unpublished doctoral dissertation, Indiana University of Pennsylvania, Indiana, PA

Shannon, P. (1992). *Becoming political: Readings and writings in the politics of literacy education.* Portsmouth, NH: Heinemann.

Shannon, P. (Ed.). (2000). If you ain't got the ABC's. *The Reading Teacher, 54*(1), 64-66.

Shannon, P. (Ed.). (2001). *Becoming political, too: New writings on the politics of literacy education.* Portsmouth, NH: Heinemann.

Smith, F. (1990). *To think.* New York: Teachers College Press.

Smith, F. (1998). *The book of learning and forgetting.* New York: Teachers College Press.

Strickland, D. S. (1994-95). Reinventing our literacy programs: Books, basics, and balance. *The Reading Teacher, 48*(4), 294-306.

Taback, S. (1997). *I know an old lady who swallowed a fly.* New York: Viking Penguin

Westcott, N. B. (1989). *Skip to my Lou.* New York: Trumpet Club.

Whitin, D., & Whitin, P. (1998). Learning is born of doubting: Cultivating a skeptical stance. *Language Arts, 76,* 123-129.

Willis, A. I., & Harris, V. J. (2000). Political acts: Literacy learning and teaching. *Reading Research Quarterly, 35*(1), 72-89.

Zemelman, S., Daniels, H., & Hyde, A. (1998). *Best practice: New standards for teaching and learning* (2nd ed.). Portsmouth, NH: Heinemann.

Chapter 8
Facilitating Transitions With Narrative and Expository Texts in Grades 2-4

Marcia F. Nash,
University of Maine at Farmington

"The universe is made up
of stories, not atoms."

—Muriel Rukeyser

The whole universe may not be made up of stories, but that part of it inhabited by primary grade children certainly is. Narrative texts dominate early elementary school. Narrative text tells a story that may be factual or fictional; the story can be told in prose or in verse. As Caswell and Duke (1998) point out, "Learning to read is often a process of learning to read fictional narrative, and learning to write is often a process of learning to write personal narrative" (p. 108). There seems to be ample justification for this emphasis on narrative. Narrative discourse plays a crucial role in discourse and literacy development, and in socialization (McCabe, 1996).

Yet the literature suggests that post-primary schoolchildren's poor performance with texts that are not in story form—such as expository texts (a form of writing that explains or sets forth information) in mathematics, science, social studies, art, music, technology, health, and other curriculum areas—may be due in part to their lack of experience with such texts (Applebee, Langer, Mullis, Latham, & Gentile, 1994; Langer, Applebee, Mullis, & Foertsch, 1990). At the same time, the information explosion demands that learners of all ages be able to comprehend expository texts in formats ranging from books to CD-ROMs to the Internet.

Negotiating narrative text is an important skill for elementary schoolchildren, since these materials are such a dominant part of classroom life. Narrative discourse also plays a key role in development, however. Limited exposure to expository text clearly has a detrimental effect on children's ability to comprehend it. Thus, at least two challenges confront the grades "before the middle years." First, it is important to build on and expand children's sense of story structure as they encounter ever more sophisticated narratives. Second, it is important to provide children with the opportunities, and the strategies, to negotiate expository text. This chapter will discuss methods and materials for expanding sense of story and ways of using narrative text to ease the transition into expository text.

Expanding the Sense of Story

With enough exposure to narrative text, children can develop a sense of story structure beginning in 1st grade (Dreher & Singer, 1980). Research in comprehension of narrative text supports the theory that readers develop a schema for story that represents their concept of how stories are typically structured (Mandler, 1983; McConaughy, 1980, 1985). Basic knowledge of setting, character, problem, and solution can help young children comprehend the stories they read or hear.

The challenge to teachers is to present children with stories that will take them beyond the structures they encounter in basic picture storybooks. The notion of setting needs to be expanded to include the concept of integral setting—a setting that is an important part of the story and that may play a part in character and/or plot development. Ideas about character need to embrace both dynamic and static characters. Simple statements of problem and solution can evolve into elements of plot, including sequence of events, conflict, goal attainment, and resolution. The concept of themes—first explicit, then implicit and secondary themes—should be introduced and explored.

Three formats can support 2nd-, 3rd-, and 4th-graders as they make the transition to more complex narratives such as sophisticated picture storybooks, stepping stone chapter books, and novellas. Illustrated stories in the form of picture storybooks are no longer just for the "learning to read" crowd. Authors and author/illustrators craft sophisticated stories with illustrations that enhance and extend the stories. Their brevity and the support provided by the illustrations make these books ideal for mini-lessons on story elements. *Rechenka's Eggs* (Polacco, 1988) and *Tar Beach* (Ringgold, 1991) are examples of picture storybooks with integral settings; the settings are absolutely necessary for character and/or plot development. *Chrysanthemum* (Henkes, 1991) and *Brave Irene* (Steig, 1986) are both stories with fully developed main characters. David Macaulay's *Black and White* (1990) and *Shortcut* (1995) could be used to study sequence and plot development. *Smoky Night* (Bunting, 1994) and *Two Bad Ants* (Van Allsburg, 1988) could be used to explore theme.

Stepping stone chapter books are the first manageable extended texts for young readers. They are intended for the youngest readers, or for readers who need the most support. Typically, they are illustrated on every page and have large print as well as simple sentence structures. They are generally episodic, which allows for extended character and plot development through manageable, semi-autonomous story segments. They often occur in series, making them convenient for independent reading and concurrent literature circles. The *Frog and Toad* series by Arnold Lobel, the *Fox* series by James Marshall, and the *Minnie and Moo* series by Denys Cazet are examples of stepping stone books that are particularly good for discussions about how authors reveal characters.

The *Young Cam Jansen* series by David Adler and the *Nate the Great* series by Marjorie Sharmat can be useful for introducing a new genre (detective/mystery) and for discussing plot development.

Chapter books for these grade levels also come in a slightly more sophisticated format, and might be called "the next step" chapter books. They vary from the basic stepping stone chapter books in that they have fewer illustrations, more text, and more sophisticated plots. Like the basic stepping stone chapter books, they are often in series. *The Werewolf Club* series by Daniel Pinkwater, the *Captain Underpants* series by Dav Pilkey, the *Time Warp Trio* series by Jon Scieszka, and the *Magic Tree House* series by Mary Pope Osborne all could be useful when discussing the structure of fantasy. Ellen Conford's *Jenny Archer* series and Barbara Park's *Junie B. Jones* series can be used to discuss character and plot development.

Novellas are short novels. They can be very similar to the "next step" chapter books, but are likely to be longer, with integral settings, fully developed characters, more complex plot structures, and implicit themes. Novellas like Lawrence Yep's *Hiroshima* (1995), Patricia MacLachlan's *Sarah, Plain and Tall* (1985), and Betsy Byars' *Tornado* (1996) are useful for introducing children to the structure of historical fiction, the notion of integral setting, or the concept of implicit theme.

Using Narrative Text To Transition Into Expository Text

Narrative and expository texts co-exist in every classroom. They can be used together to enhance and extend each other and the curriculum. McMackin (1998) suggests that narrative picture books can be used to introduce expository structures—such as description, compare/contrast, sequence, cause and effect—because in many narrative picture books these expository structures underlie the narration. For example, *Grandfather and I* (Buckley, 1994) is a narrative text with a compare/contrast pattern. It could be used in conjunction with expository text such as *Outside and Inside Trees* (Markle, 1993) or *Horns, Antlers, Fangs, and Tusks* (Rauzon, 1993) to explore that pattern. Other expository text patterns accessible through narrative text are description/numeration, cause and effect, problem/solution, and sequence.

Lauritzen and Jaeger (1997) propose a "narrative curriculum" in which "a rich and compelling story with a universal theme" (p. xiii) is used to organize the curriculum. In this curriculum, readers interact with a story and develop inquiries based on those interactions. The inquiries lead naturally into social studies, science, language arts, mathematics, art, music, technology, and other curriculum areas. As an example of this approach, Lauritzen and Jaeger (1997) describe a cycle of curriculum that they developed with elementary school students based on the story *Very Last First Time* (Andrews, 1985). This story of an Inuit girl's adventure gathering mussels under the ice of a frozen bay led to a week-long unit in which the students studied "Inuit culture, arctic geography and climate, the nature of ice and tides, how candles burn, mathematical problem solving, model building, and the biology and nutrition of mussels" (p. 21). The narrative text provided the context for explorations using a variety of expository texts and other resources.

Caswell and Duke (1998) believe the traditional argument that children need to be prepared for the shift toward expository text, which seems to occur by 4th grade, is not the only reason to infuse such texts into the lower grades. In their work with children at the Harvard Literacy Laboratory, they have found that some children who do not become engaged with stories will respond positively to expository text. The "narrative curriculum" would provide a context for using expository text with these children.

The curricular and book recommendations in this chapter are intended to show how narrative text can facilitate transitions in the 2nd, 3rd, and 4th grades in two ways: by building on and expanding children's sense of story structure as they encounter ever more sophisticated narratives, and by providing children with opportunities to negotiate expository text and the strategies to do so. A classroom can be a universe "made up of stories," a place that invites exploration of the concept of story and also provides opportunities to interact with expository text.

References

Applebee, A. N., Langer, J. A., Mullis, I. V., Latham, A. S., & Gentile, C. A. (1994). *NAESP 1992 writing report card* (Report No. 23-W01). Washington, DC: U.S. Government Printing Office.

Caswell, L. J., & Duke, N. K. (1998). Non-narrative as a catalyst for literacy development. *Language Arts, 75*, 108-117.

Dreher, M. J., & Singer, H. (1980). Story grammar instruction unnecessary for intermediate grade students. *The Reading Teacher, 33*, 261-268.

Langer, J. A., Applebee, A. N., Mullis, I. V., & Foertsch, M. A. (1990). *Learning to read in our nation's schools: Instruction and achievement in 1988 at grades 4, 8, and 12.* Princeton, NJ: Educational Testing Services.

Lauritzen, C., & Jaeger, M. (1997). *Integrating learning through story: The narrative curriculum.* Albany, NY: Delmar.

Mandler, J. M. (1983). *Stories: The function of structure.* Washington, DC: National Science Foundation. (EDRS Publication No. ED 238-247)

McCabe, A. (1996). *Chameleon readers: Teaching children to appreciate all kinds of good stories.* New York: McGraw-Hill.

McConaughy, S. H. (1980). Using story structure in the classroom. *Language Arts, 57*, 157-164.

McConaughy, S. H. (1985). Good and poor readers' comprehension of story structure across different input and output modalities. *Reading Research Quarterly, 20*, 219-232.

McMackin, M. C. (1998). Using narrative picture books to build awareness of expository text structure. *Reading Horizons, 39*, 7-20.

Children's Literature

Individual Titles

Andrews, J. (1985). *Very last first time.* New York: Atheneum.

Bunting, E. (1994). *Smoky night.* San Diego, CA: Harcourt.

Buckley, H. (1994). *Grandfather and I.* New York: Lothrop, Lee, & Shepard.

Byars, B. (1996). *Tornado.* New York: HarperCollins.

Henkes, K. (1991). *Chrysanthemum.* New York: Greenwillow.

Macaulay, D. (1990). *Black and white.* Boston: Houghton Mifflin.

Macaulay, D. (1999). *Shortcut.* Boston: Houghton Mifflin.

MacLachlan, P. (1985). *Sarah, plain and tall.* New York: Harper.

Markle, S. (1993). *Outside and inside trees.* New York: Bradbury Press.

Polacco, P. (1988). *Rechenka's eggs.* New York: Philomel.

Rauzon, M. (1993). *Horns, antlers, fangs, and tusks.* New York: Lothrop, Lee & Shepard.

Ringgold, F. (1991). *Tar beach.* New York: Crown.

Steig, W. (1996). *Brave Irene.* New York: Farrar Straus & Giroux.

Van Allsburg, C. (1988). *Two bad ants.* Boston: Houghton Mifflin.

Yep, L. (1995). *Hiroshima.* New York: Scholastic.

Children's Literature: Series

Adler, D. *Cam Jansen series*. New York: Puffin.

Adler, D. *Young Cam Jansen series*. New York: Viking Children's Books.

Cazet, D. *Minnie and Moo series*. DK Publishing.

Conford, E. *Jenny Archer series*. Boston: Little, Brown.

Lobel, A. *Frog and Toad series*. New York: HarperCollins.

Marshall, J. *Fox series*. New York: Penguin.

Park, B. *Junie B. Jones series*. New York: Random House.

Pilkey, D. *Captain Underpants series*. New York: Scholastic

Pinkwater, D. *The Werewolf Club series*. New York: Aladdin.

Osborne, M. *Magic Treehouse series*. New York: Random House.

Scieszka, J. *The Time Warp Trio series*. New York: Puffin.

Sharmat, M. *Nate the Great series*. New York: Young Yearling.

Chapter 9
Tearing Down the Walls That Divide:
School and Community Partnerships in the Teaching of Reading and Writing

Michelle Kelley,
FLaRE Center, University of Central Florida

Sue Wilder,
Seminole County, Florida, Public Schools

"Amazing things happen when two people sit down and share a good book. Relationships form, connections are made, and words come alive! I can't wait to find out what happens at the end of the story we are reading."
—Tara, Red Bug Reads Tutor

This quote came from a journal entry written by a preservice teacher during the semester she served as a tutor in the Red Bug Reads program. Walk through Red Bug Elementary School in Casselberry, Florida, and you will see tutors and students reading, writing, and learning together. Many of the tutors, like Tara, are University of Central Florida students. Others are parents of Red Bug children, senior citizens, or civic-minded community volunteers. All have joined together with school personnel to support struggling readers.

Consider the possibilities for success if every child having difficulty reading received individual assistance from a trained tutor. It was this idea that prompted the development of a one-on-one tutoring program for our 3rd-, 4th-, and 5th-graders who were having trouble with reading. In this chapter, we will outline the details of how this project was developed, the resulting benefits for students, and how its implementation serves to tear down some of the walls that exist in education.

Background

In 1995, our school began focusing on several literacy initiatives to better meet the needs of our diverse and growing population. These initiatives included a literacy support teacher in 2nd grade, several primary tutoring programs, and an intervention inclusion classroom for 5th-grade students. In spite of these successful interventions, a great number of intermediate students were still reading below grade level. Many of these students were new to Red Bug and many appeared to have oral language deficiencies, showed evidence of physical and mental disabilities, spoke English as a second language, or had been diagnosed with attention deficit hyperactivity disorder (ADHD).

Often, struggling intermediate readers can *read* all of the words. Their difficulties lie in grasping meaning from text (Weaver, 1988). Vacca and Padak (1990) have identified several criteria to

59

describe what it means to be at-risk in reading. Some students who are at-risk struggle with the social and academic aspects of reading. Other students do not understand the purpose of reading. They may be unable to monitor comprehension or have limited strategies. Some at-risk readers lack the skills needed to use reading to learn, and some lack the cognitive skills for handling text demands. Other struggling readers avoid reading, even though they possess the cognitive skills needed to read. Our tutoring framework was developed to combat these problems, particularly in the area of comprehension.

Traditional reading interventions target primary children, and Red Bug Elementary School has several such initiatives in place. The aim of Red Bug Reads is to provide support for older students who are having difficulty with reading. While regular classroom teachers do their best to meet the needs of all students, they are limited in the amount of time they can devote to individual assistance. This project complements teachers' efforts by providing much-needed one-on-one help for those children who could benefit most.

Framework for Tutoring

In our roles at Red Bug, we work primarily with struggling readers. Each of us could identify several students who needed reading support that was unavailable to them. Agreeing that these students would benefit from tutoring, we researched many different tutoring programs (Morrow & Walker, 1997; Pinnell & Fountas, 1997). The original tutoring framework we created reflects best practices in reading instruction (Zemelman, Daniels, & Hyde, 1998). The model is highly structured, but organized in a way to allow for flexibility and choice, according to the needs of children and the tutors' level of experience.

Fortunately, many civic-minded individuals in the community volunteered to assist children with reading. However, we found that very few of them have the background and experience necessary to guide children who are having difficulty with learning. To ensure success for both children and the tutors, we felt it imperative that this tutoring model be both practical and effective (see Figure 1). The tutoring session is designed to last approximately 45 minutes. Each component of the framework is allotted a certain amount of time, although this is flexible to respect the tutor's and student's individual needs.

The framework enables students to build good comprehension skills by using before-, during-, and after-reading strategies that are easily demonstrated and practiced. Each student has a two-pocket folder that is housed alphabetically in a file cabinet easily accessible to tutors. Inside the folder is a student journal, a copy of the tutoring framework, a book log, a tutoring form, and some copies of various graphic organizers to enhance comprehension.

Before reading, the tutor helps a student activate prior knowledge, make predictions, and set a purpose for reading. In the "Read Together" part of the tutoring session, the options include having the student read alone, having the tutor and student read together, and taking turns reading. These options provide the student with a model for, and practice with, good fluency and phrasing.

After reading, the tutor and student discuss the story by focusing on open-ended questions printed on the tutoring framework as a guidepost for their conversations. They also may complete a graphic organizer to aid the students in retelling the story. The tutors have access to numerous graphic organizers, which are maintained in pocket folders and displayed in our tutoring room. Before, during, and after reading, there is an optional wordwork/vocabulary segment for tutors.

After reading, the next segment is "Write Together." "Write Together" also offers options: Write Side by Side; I Write, You Write; and Written Dialogue. Extra journals are kept in the tutoring room so that tutors and students can write side by side on an agreed-upon topic.

The collection of books used in this project includes many titles related to grade level, content areas, and children's interests. Many of the books are easier to read than those found in the children's regular classrooms, facilitating success. Tutors are trained in the use of our school's Guided Reading Resource Library, where books are sorted by reading level, in order to provide students with

RED BUG READS TUTORING FRAMEWORK, PART 1

1. Rereading Familiar Passages or Quick Write About a Book   5-10 minutes

Tutoring sessions should begin with the student reading a short passage from a familiar book or completing a quick write about a book they have read or are still reading. The familiar rereading can be his/her favorite part, a section they found amusing or interesting, a part that was particularly special to them (something that reminded them of their own lives, etc.) or a part that was confusing. Spend a few minutes discussing the section read. Please record the title on the tutoring form. The quick write can include any of the above but also the possible questions for a response log (see sheets).

2. Read Together   15-20 minutes

Choosing Books: Using the student's assessment information, select several books at an appropriate reading level. Ask your student to select several titles he or she would like to read. These books should be kept in the student's browsing box. He/she should decide on one of these books to read today, and the others will be read in subsequent sessions. After all the books have been read you will need to repeat this process.

Before Reading: Set a purpose for the reading. Have students make a prediction about the book. Review the title of the story and leaf through the book looking at the pictures. Discuss what might happen in the book. You might say, "Let's look at the title and cover and try to guess what this story might be about." Please record the title of the new book on the tutoring form.

During Reading Choose From the Following Options:

Option 1 - *Read Together.* Read a couple of pages aloud modeling fluency and phrasing to convey the meaning of the story (have the student follow the text you are reading with their eyes). As you read stop to ask, "What do you think will happen next?" Etc... When the student is ready, ask him/her to take over the reading or share the reading for the remainder of the book (If the book is too hard and the child is struggling, go ahead and read the story aloud to him/her).

Option 2 - *Student Reads.* Have the student read the book alone. This could be done silently or aloud. If the student is reading silently, break the book into short passages so that you can discuss the book during the reading. You may want to have the student read only part of the book alone and then take turns if this process is taking too long.

Option 3 - *Taking Turns.* Take turns reading, with each of you reading a paragraph or a page. Discuss the book as you are reading.

After Reading:

- After you finish the reading, discuss the story by asking open-ended questions. **Choose one or two** of the possible questions for response logs-listed separately. For informational books you might ask: What information that we read did you already know? What new information did you learn? What do you still want to learn more about?

- Use a graphic organizer to help retell the story. Choose a graphic organizer (see examples in the training handout). This can be completed together or by the student alone. This may take more than one session to fill out, keep this work with other tutoring documents.

Figure 1

reading material at their instructional level. The children and tutors select the books together, thereby modeling and practicing book selection.

Rogers and Renard (1999) report that teachers can enhance a student's motivation to learn by fulfilling their emotional needs: "Students are motivated when they believe that teachers care about them personally and educationally" (p. 34). This project seeks to enhance student motivation and comprehension. Tutors are given strategies for scaffolding children in each tutoring session, resulting in a successful reading experience. After scaffolding the student, the tutor encourages the student to self-monitor and become independent. Thus, children gain confidence and become more motivated to read (Keefe & Jenkins, 1997). In order to provide continuity, the tutor-tutee relationship continues for a minimum of one semester, but usually spans the entire school year.

Each tutoring session ends with the tutor completing a blank tutoring form (see Figure 2).

This form mirrors the tutoring framework and provides guidance for the tutor, without interrupting the flow of the tutoring session. It also gives the tutor and child the opportunity to reflect and develop goals for the next tutoring session. The forms also are used as a means of communicating with the facilitators, who read the forms each week, respond to the tutors' and children's questions, and provide specific praise and feedback. This dialogue allows us to monitor the project and helps maintain a sense of teamwork.

Implementation and Training

At the beginning of each year, a meeting is scheduled with 3rd-, 4th-, and 5th-grade teachers to review the project and begin identifying children who might benefit from participating. Once teachers get to know their students and have the opportunity to review their records from previous years, they compile a list of potential candidates for tutoring. These children are evaluated using the

---

3. Write Together 15-20 minutes

Option 1 - *Writing Side by Side.* Before writing, determine what you want to write about. After brainstorming ideas, write in your journal as you sit side by side. You each have a journal and you write for five or more minutes and then share what you have written with each other.

Option 2 - *I Write, You Write.* Together, select a topic to write about. Using the topic selected, begin writing in the child's journal. You begin by writing for one minute. Read what you wrote and talk about what might come next. Have the child write the next sentence. Keep alternating sentences and sharing what has been written and what should come next. When the story is complete, read the story together. Revise any parts as necessary.

Option 3 - *Written Dialogue.* Write a comment or question to the child. The child reads what you wrote and writes an answer or response. Read the child's response and then write a comment about what the child wrote, and so on. This is like a silent conversation. Use your judgment as to how many times each of you should respond.

4. Word Work/Vocabulary (optional) 10 minutes

This could come before, during, or after reading. These could be words that they will encounter in their reading or words they encountered while reading. You may wish to do some type of making words modification or other vocabulary building activities.

5. Reflective Questions 5 minutes

With the student, fill out the "Reflective Questions..." portion of the tutoring form once a week. You might use one or two of the recommended questions to help students reflect.

Figure 1, continued

Developmental Reading Assessment (DRA) to determine reading levels and strategies used when reading. Classroom teachers provide this information to the tutors.

Tutors are recruited through targeted brochures and as a part of the school's overall volunteer program. University students enrolled in undergraduate language arts courses are invited to participate as part of their course requirements. Volunteers are asked to commit at least one hour per week, per child for this program. Training sessions are scheduled once a month for any new tutors and are conducted individually or in small groups. If volunteers are unable to attend one of the scheduled training sessions, accommodations are made to fit tutors' schedules.

The activities used in the training sessions are designed to build an understanding of the reading process, familiarize the tutors with the lesson plans and other tools to be used, and provide them with practical tips and suggestions for making this experience a success for both them and the stu-

---

Developing Readers Tutoring Form

Student Name _____ Tutor Name _____

Home School _____ Date _____

Please fill in the appropriate blanks and check off activities you completed together.

1. **Familiar Re-reading or Quick Write**   **5 minutes**
   _____

Title of book_____ Level _____

2. **Read Together**   **15-20 minutes**
   • **Set a Purpose, Predict, and Preview Book**   _____
   • **Select one of the following:**
       Option 1 - Read Together   _____
       Option 2 - Student Reads   _____
       Option 3 - Taking Turns   _____
   • **Discuss the book, complete a response log**
     question or complete graphic organizer   _____

Title of new book _____ Level _____

3. **Write Together**   **15-20 minutes**
   • **Select one of the following:**
       Option 1 - Writing Side by Side   _____
       Option 2 - I Write, You Write   _____
       Option 3 - Written Dialogue   _____

4. **Word Work/Vocabulary (Optional)**   **10 minutes**
   _____

5. **Reflective Questions (Complete once a week)**   **5 minutes**
   • **What did you learn this week that you didn't know last week?**
   • **How will you use what you learned this week in school?**
   • **What do you hope to learn next week?**

Figure 1, continued

dents. During the training, the tutors participate in several reading experiences themselves, using some of the books and graphic organizers available to them for tutoring. At the end of the training, they are given a tour of the school and meet the student(s) and their classroom teachers.

In addition to the on-campus training, tutors from the university receive training as part of their coursework. Each semester, one class session is dedicated to Red Bug Reads training. During this three-hour session, the students learn about the background of and rationale for the project and receive the same training provided to other tutors. The collaborating professor offers these students the opportunity to serve as tutors in lieu of other assignments. The students learn to create a book packet using the tutoring format—a course requirement for all students. The books used can be selected from the Red Bug Reads collection or any other source available to the students. Once the book packet is developed, the students try it out with children or their classmate peers. They make revisions based on these experiences and compile a final copy. These book packets are available to all tutors and teachers at the school.

Outcomes

A variety of assessment tools, including standardized reading tests, surveys, and informal observations, allow us to evaluate the success of the tutoring program. Reading assessments demonstrate, on average, more than a full year's growth for the students receiving tutoring. Specific areas of improvement include the ability to: make predictions, read with phrasing and fluency, comprehend written text, monitor errors, use problem-solving strategies, and make connections from the known to the unknown.

Each semester, classroom teachers, participating children, tutors, and university students fill out a survey to evaluate the project and obtain suggestions for improvement. Survey results from all groups remain extremely positive and encouraging. When asked if the project should be continued, one teacher responded, "Heck yeah, you better! These kids need the one-on-one attention to achieve the leaps and bounds they have displayed

this year!" This quote is representative of the feedback received from teachers regarding the project. They cite the following significant improvements in their students' reading: better fluency, better word recognition, improved comprehension, more critical reading, and use of word attack skills. In addition, teachers note that students are able to follow directions better, work more quickly, are better organized, participate more in classroom discussions, and even volunteer to read aloud—something they rarely did before. All of the teachers want the project to continue; their only suggestion for improvement being an increase in the number of volunteers.

Tutor surveys indicate that they enjoy tutoring, and some continue to participate for several years. They find the training and support extremely beneficial, and mention numerous personal benefits we had not considered. Many of the volunteers specify the value of having the opportunity to learn about other cultures and family traditions. Some of them say they learned new ways to communicate with children, including their own. One tutor indicated that the experience added another perspective to her view of how children learn to read. As a result, she felt she had really made a difference for the children she tutored. Another volunteer voiced her finding that tutoring "inspired me to further my own reading and writing." Another felt the experience "made me a better parent." Still another wrote, "I have cherished my experience and hope to be a part of Red Bug Reads in the future."

"I can read better." "I can read harder books." "I have more confidence in myself." "I like to read now." "I understand more." These are a few of the responses children give when asked how Red Bug Reads benefited them. Students respond positively to the question, "Have you enjoyed having a tutor?" Responses include: "I had the chance to learn more." "I get to read the books I like to read." "It was fun, and it helped me with my reading." and "I like having help." When asked for their ideas on improving the project, students suggested that we include spelling lessons, hire more tutors, meet more often, and make the tutoring sessions longer. One student's response to whether we should continue the project demonstrates the power of this intervention: "Yes, because it can help my brother, just like it helped me."

The evaluation surveys from the University of Central Florida students have been overwhelmingly positive. This note, written on the final day of tutoring, typifies their response: "I have enjoyed my time at Red Bug, and seeing Nikki improve. Next year, I plan to take fewer classes and I hope to be able to help again with the Red Bug Reads program. Thank you for the time you have invested in me. I have learned just as much as Nikki."

After three years of implementation, the out-comes of this project have far exceeded our expectations. Preservice teachers have gained skills that will serve them as they become teachers. Community members have cherished the opportunity to serve and learn from students. Teachers have received assistance for the children who need it the most. And, most important, participating students' reading has improved, as has their classroom performance and self-confidence.

Tearing Down the Walls

Just like walls in buildings, the walls in education act as barriers to keep some things in and others out. These walls take on many different forms. At

---

RED BUG READS TUTORING FORM

Student's Name _____   Tutor's Name _____

Teacher's Name _____   Date _____

Please fill in the appropriate blanks and check off the activities you completed together.

1. **Familiar Re-reading (if applicable)**   **5 minutes**
   or choose a new book to read.

Title of Book _____ Level (if available) _____

2. **Read Together**   **15-20 minutes**
   - **Preview book**   _____
   - **Select one of the following for session:**
       Option 1 - Read Together   _____
       Option 2 - Student Reads   _____
       Option 3 - Taking Turns   _____
   - **Discuss the book &/or complete a**   _____
     graphic organizer (can be the write together too)

3. **Write Together**   **15-20 minutes**
   - **Select one of the following:**
       Option 1 - Writing Side by Side   _____
       Option 2 - I Write, You Write   _____
       Option 3 - Written Dialogue   _____

4. **Reflect and Set Goals**   **5 minutes**
   Today we.............

Next time we will work on ....

Figure 2

the school level, walls separate effective and ineffective readers. There are instructional walls within the classroom, dividing struggling and advanced learners. There are curriculum walls, creating unreasonable academic demands on students and teachers. Far too often, there are walls between teachers and within and across grade levels.

Tomlinson and Kalbfleisch (1998) argue that few modifications for struggling learners are made in classrooms driven by the belief that there is too much to cover and too little time to cover the content required by curricular demands. "A one-size-fits-all approach to classroom teaching is ineffective for most students and harmful to some" (p. 52). Because curriculum demands in the intermediate grades are vast and content materials often are written at or above grade level, many struggling readers lose confidence in their abilities. When these children have only minimal opportunities to experience success, they eventually shut down or develop behavior problems.

We believe that, in some cases, the wall most in need of being torn down is that which exists between schools and colleges of education. While practicing teachers have much to offer their future colleagues, they do not usually have the opportunity to do so until students are near graduation. Likewise, university professors and their students have much to offer practicing teachers and could make an impact in ways that improve teaching and learning.

Opportunities for firsthand interactions with children that are directly related to course work are unusual for undergraduate education majors. "Future elementary teachers receive only a basic introduction to reading. The reading course may comprise as little as one-tenth of the future teacher's academic program during one year of college" (Anderson, Hiebert, Scott, & Wilkinson, 1985, p. 106). Many preservice training programs do not give teachers the needed preparation and training to support struggling readers (Duffy-Hester, 1999). Schools seldom reach out to colleges of education for assistance, and many future teachers have limited experiences in schools prior

to their final student teaching internships. A secondary goal of this project is to give college students a window into their future as educators, as well as the opportunity to create a book packet that will be useful to them in their own classrooms and to the Red Bug Reads tutors. "We need to instill the confidence, knowledge, and will in pre-service and practicing teachers to teach struggling readers" (Duffy-Hester, 1999, p. 492).

All of these walls make it difficult for schools and communities to collaborate in ways that are beneficial to students. Through the Red Bug Reads project, we believe we have begun to chip away at some of the walls that divide; we consider the success of this project a demonstration of the power of a community partnership. More important, this project provides children with the opportunity to bond with a joyfully literate adult—something Shirley Brice Heath suggests is the single most important condition for literacy learning. We agree!

References

Anderson, R. C., Hiebert, E. H., Scott, J. A., & Wilkinson, I. A. (1985). *Becoming a nation of readers. The report of the Commission on Reading.* Washington, DC: National Institute of Education.

Duffy-Hester, A. M. (1999). Teaching struggling readers in elementary classrooms: A review of classroom reading programs and principles for instruction. *The Reading Teacher, 52,* 480-495.

Keefe, J., & Jenkins, J. (1997). *Instruction and the learning environment.* Larchmont, NY: Eye on Education.

Morrow, L. M., & Walker, B. J. (1997). *The reading team: A handbook for volunteer tutors K-3.* Newark, DE: International Reading Association.

Pinnell, G. S., & Fountas, I. (1997). *Help America read: Coordinator's guide.* Portsmouth, NH: Heinemann.

Rogers, S., & Renard, L. (1999). Relationship-driven teaching. *Educational Leadership, 57,* 34-37.

Tomlinson, C., & Kalbfleisch, M. (1998). Teach me, teach my brain: A call for differentiated classrooms. *Educational Leadership, 56,* 52-55.

Vacca, R., & Padak, N. (1990). Who's at risk in reading? *Journal of Reading, 33,* 486-488.

Weaver, C. (1988). *Reading process and practice: From socio-psycholinguistics to whole language.* Portsmouth, NH: Heinemann.

Zemelman, S., Daniels, H., & Hyde, A. (1998). *Best practice: New standards for teaching and learning in America's schools* (2nd ed.). Portsmouth, NH: Reed Publishing.

Writing World

Chapter 10
Creating an Author's Notebook:
Ending Writing Welfare As We Know It

Sherron Killingsworth Roberts,
University of Central Florida

How often do teachers hear this heartfelt cry, "But Teacher, I don't know what to write about!"? Donald Graves (1976, 1983) coined the phrase "writing welfare" to describe the way that some teachers attempt to help children become better writers. In the midst of the creative writing push of the 1970s and early 1980s, when many teachers fed their students catchy sentence starters or clever scenarios, Graves argued that teachers should avoid force-feeding topics to children. In his mind, this "writing welfare" could arrest students' development toward finding their own voices. On the other hand, some teachers tell students right away that they will have to be in charge of their own writing topics. In this case, students not only complain "I don't know what to write about," but also use this initial roadblock as an excuse not to write at all.

Donald Murray advises writers who are stymied to "start by writing about something you know. . . . You can't write about nothing" (Murray, in Graves, 1983, p. 12). Another great author, Lucy Calkins (1991), suggests building a notebook of ideas, not only as a tool for writing, but also as a tool for living. Jean Little (1987) notes that by compiling these ideas drawn from your own life experiences, it is possible to see the cumulative effect and realize that "your thoughts, your noticings, your fleet of orange slices matter" (pp. 92-93).

When we start to bring our students into alignment with authors' circles (as outlined by Harste, Woodard, & Burke, 1984), students model themselves after real-life authors. They begin to see the recursive process of brainstorming ideas, and of writing and rewriting and turning and twisting ideas inside and out.

The Author's Notebook

This article outlines the concept of an author's notebook (or idea bank); it is borrowed from many prolific writers for use in the elementary classroom. Of course, writers of all ages could benefit. In order to end "writing welfare" as we know it and give credence and power to the voice of children, I suggest that teachers allow students to create these author's notebooks. To begin creating and thinking like a real author, I show my students examples of various author's notebooks. I have one example that is kept on index cards in an old recipe file. I have another from a student that was collected in a layer book, with each layer representing a section. And I tell them about yet another example that was made using a HyperStudio stack, with links to each section. Whatever format this compilation of ideas takes, the author's notebook should contain some of the following elements: character names, interesting places, problems to solve, quotations, overheard conversations, and any other helpful categories.

Elementary students can follow in the footsteps of prolific authors by compiling ideas that will help them overcome the intimidation of facing a blank page or blank computer screen. After helping children in grades 3 to 8 in workshop settings to create their own author's notebooks, my suggestion would be to have a mini-lesson concerning the importance of each of the following headings and then offer resources in a learning station format.

• **Character Names Section.** In my classes, we discuss the importance of giving characters names that suit the characteristics of that person or that highlight some character trait that we want the reader to be sure to find. I discuss the intrigue and implications of a character named Harlan Granger in *Roll of Thunder, Hear My Cry* (Taylor, 1976), as well as the character of Salamanca Tree Hiddle in *Walk Two Moons* (Creech, 1994). Even those who have not read about these characters might be able to venture a guess as to what sort of role they might play, what sort of people they are, and why the author would choose these intriguing names for their characters. After providing that rationale and motivation for creating meaningful character names, the students have the opportunity to take their index cards, eMates, or layer books to a learning station that has resources to help them begin compiling a list of interesting names to use in their upcoming writing. The resources I have found most useful are various baby name books and old phone books. In fact, my own author's notebook contains a character name that I still would like to develop into a satirical piece called "The Reverend Pat Answers."

• **Interesting Places Section.** Sometimes, before students start to collect ideas for interesting places, it helps to have a mini-lesson on choosing between an integral setting versus a more universal setting. To inspire students to think of unusual places, I have stocked a related learning station with travel magazines, maps (*Family Fun* magazine always has a section on traveling for children), lists of related Internet sites, and a book called *Books on the Move* (Knorr & Espeland, 1997) that describes both interesting places for families as well as related children's books. Generally, students will record various interesting places that they can work into future writing. Students always are encouraged to add their own experiences and ideas to the mix. As I search for a new idea in a book or magazine, I

often am drawn to memories of houses and rooms and towns that I have left behind. Children should be encouraged to document any and all ideas in their author's notebooks for later use.

• **Problems To Solve Section.** "Problems to solve" is such an important heading for authors that over the years I have found several ways to help students find their own ideas for this section. In many cases, I find that a week-long unit on the importance of incorporating conflict into writing will help. I generally start with identifying the conflict in well-known fairy or folktales or in popular picture books. Having made clear to my students the need for conflict or a problem, I provide several very different ways for them to collect problems, including the following:

Comic strips. One fun way to collect problems is to provide comic strips for students to read. I have found that elementary students lose momentum when given whole pages of the comics or "funnies"; therefore, I cut them into individual comic strips in order to maintain the students' focus. Often, students will select several comics that present an interesting problem to solve, and they will simply glue or paste these comics onto their index cards or in their layer books. Sometimes students elaborate upon and extend the simple text of the selected comic, but many times I have been reminded of a similar problem in my own life about which I will later choose to write.

Want ads. Another great vehicle for generating ideas about problems to solve are the want ads. Students find this an interesting and motivating resource. I cut out many different want ads; the lost and found ads, in particular, yield the most interesting problems. Students are instructed to read the lost and found ads, and then brainstorm possible scenarios that created the need for the advertisement. I remember reading an advertisement in our local newspaper that announced a sum of cash being found near our university. My students and I not only imagined the personality of the person who would place such an ad, but also brainstormed about the unscrupulous folks who might try to claim the money even though they were not the rightful owners. We even generated story ideas that described the possible scams that might emerge from this scenario.

Writing prompts. In the creative writing movement of the 1970s and 1980s, many teachers gave students independent task cards that had a creative, sometimes wacky or "far-out," idea as a story starter. For example, a card might ask students to imagine and write about what it would be like to be transformed into the teacher. Even though these "writing prompts" are the very thing that started the whole "writing welfare" controversy, I have found that allowing students to sort through reams of old creative writing prompts can be very effective. In my mind, one of the most stimulating parts of being an author often is coming up with the "idea," whereas the actual writing process can be tedious or laborious. Invariably, students who sift through these crazy ideas (such as being a flea spying on a dog) generate—and own—new writing ideas!

• **Quotations Section.** In order to inspire students to use quotations or proverbs in their writing, or to influence their prewriting thoughts, I read portions of Madeleine L'Engle's *A Wrinkle in Time* (1962). Another great book that uses quotations is *Walk Two Moons* (Creech, 1994). Remind students that even so-called clichés, such as "Never judge a man until you've walked two moons in his moccasins," can be absolutely memorable and effective in their writing. During the mini-lesson, we discuss how these quotations emphasize the related themes of each book. I love showing students examples of how a good quote can inspire ideas, link ideas, and drive home the book's central themes. Then, I make available in a learning station many different sources for quotes, such as the Internet sites of *Bartlett's Familiar Quotations* (www.bartleby.com/99) and the *Quotation Board* (use AOL keyword "TBR," which stands for the Bookreporter); the *Scholastic Treasury of Quotations for Children* (Betz, 1998); *The New Dictionary of Thoughts* (Browns, 1961); and the series of books by Roger and McWilliams (1990, 1991, 1992), which have an abundance of stimulating and clever quotations on almost every page.

• **Overheard Conversations Section.** I have not decided what it is in my own personality that loves to eavesdrop on people, but, for better or worse,

this "hobby" can produce a rich set of ideas for the budding writer. In my own author's notebook, I have documented for future reference many different scenarios—some funny or clever, and some poignant or intriguing. About eight years ago, I overheard my college roommate asking her toddler son how many pieces of candy he wanted. Without blinking an eye, he emphatically told her "too many"!

On a recent occasion, I overheard a mother who, while introducing her son, mentioned his ADD diagnosis, as well as his subsequent retention in 1st grade. The son's smile faded as his mother introduced his siblings with much more evident pride. I have these memorable conversations noted in my Overheard Conversations Section, and I know that I will incorporate them into my writing. By being totally observant and taking in their surroundings, students will be able to breathe life into stale characters or indifferent situations. In a related station, students can bring in transcripts of overheard conversation upon which you can build a mini-lesson, as well as a subsequent small-group brainstorming and remembering session.

Conclusion

Perhaps all this information about creating an author's notebook or idea bank will inspire you or your students to find other headings or avenues for conquering "writing welfare." Some teachers find it useful to have sections that include mini-lessons attended, or to include sections listing spelling demons or transitional phrases. The idea is to make this author's notebook work for you. As teachers, we know we should end the practice of providing writing assignments that are artificial and disconnected from students' lives. Forcing students to write without providing support through an author's notebook or idea bank, however, seems equally unreasonable. Calkins notes that

> throughout the field of teaching writing, one educator after another has begun to advocate that students jot down things they notice and wonder about, their memories and ideas, their favorite words and responses to reading into a container of some sort. Donald Murray

speaks of that container as a day book, Donald Graves as a journal, Betsy Byars as a bureau drawer, and my colleagues and I as a writer's notebook. . . . (Calkins, 1994, p. 24).

Supporting our students as they shape these "containers" will serve as an important means for ending "writing welfare."

References and Resources

Adolph, J. (Executive Ed.). (1999). *Family Fun Magazine.* Northampton, MA: Family Fun Publishers.

Atwell, N. (1987). *In the middle: Writing, reading, and learning with adolescents.* Portsmouth, NH: Heinemann.

Betz, A. (Ed.). (1998). *Scholastic treasury of quotations for children.* New York: Scholastic.

Browns, R. E. (1961). *The new dictionary of thoughts* (Rev. ed.). New York: Standard Publishing.

Calkins, L. M., with Harwayne, S. (1991). *Living between the lines.* Portsmouth, NH: Heinemann.

Calkins, L. M. (1994). *The art of teaching writing.* Portsmouth, NH: Heinemann.

Creech, S. (1994). *Walk two moons.* New York: HarperTrophy.

Graves, D. H. (1976). *Let's get rid of the welfare mess in the teaching of writing.* Paper presented at the Annual Meeting of the National Conference on Language Arts in the Elementary School, Atlanta. ERIC Document ED 120 755

Graves, D. H. (1983). *Writing: Teachers and children at work.* Portsmouth, NH: Heinemann.

Graves, D. H. (1994). *A fresh look at writing.* Portsmouth, NH: Heinemann.

Harste, J. C., Woodard, V. A., & Burke, C. L. (1984). *Language stories and literacy lessons.* Portsmouth, NH: Heinemann.

Knorr, M., & Espeland, P. (1997). *Books on the move: A read-about-it, go-there guide to America's best family vacations.* St. Paul, MN: Free Spirit.

L'Engle, M. (1962). *A wrinkle in time.* New York: Farrar, Straus, & Giroux.

Little, J. (1987). *Little by little.* Ontario: Puffin.

Roger, J., & McWilliams, P. (1990). *Life 101: Everything we wish we had learned in school, but didn't.* Los Angeles: Prelude.

Roger, J., & McWilliams, P. (1991). *Do it!: Let's get off our butts.* Los Angeles: Prelude.

Roger, J., & McWilliams, P. (1992). *Wealth 101: Wealth is much more than money.* Los Angeles: Prelude.

Roller, C. M. (1996). *Variability, not disability: Struggling readers in a workshop classroom.* Newark, DE: International Reading Association.

Short, K. G., Harste, J. C., & Burke, C. (1996). *Creating classrooms for authors and inquirers* (2nd ed.). Portsmouth, NH: Heinemann.

Taylor, M. D. (1976). *Roll of thunder, hear my cry.* New York: Puffin.

Chapter 11
Authors in the Making:
An Invitation To Join the Writer's Club

Patricia A. Crawford,
University of Central Florida

Stephen Schroeder,
Volusia County Schools, Florida

"Slant up, slant down
and draw a line,
Slant up, slant down
and draw a line,
Slant up, slant down
and draw a line,
To make a capital A."

This song, a short ditty sung to the tune of "Here We Go 'Round the Mulberry Bush," is a relic of bygone days. Originally taught to 1st-graders, it was intended to remind young writers about the basics of letter formation. The song captured a view of the composition process that was governed first by the rules of manuscript formation and then by the nuances of cursive writing.

It seems that the formal writing curriculum of the past had little to do with constructing meaning, sharing knowledge, or collaborating with peers. Rather, it had everything to do with sitting quietly and carefully copying script from the board. From time to time, students would have

the opportunity to engage in creative writing. Experiences that allowed young writers to develop and refine full pieces of original text, however, were decidedly limited. Educators paid little attention to the actual composition process, and opportunities to develop a genuine sense of what it meant to be an author were more the exception than the rule.

Our understanding of children's writing and the nature of the writing process has changed greatly. Decades of research on elementary students' writing have revealed something that should have been apparent all along: If children are going to be successful writers, they need to have ongoing opportunities to write in purposeful, authentic, and meaningful ways (Calkins, 1994; Graves, 1983; Short, Harste, & Burke, 1996). Like all writers, students need a sense of ownership over their work. They need opportunities to revisit works in process as they rehearse, draft, revise, and edit text en route to creating a final draft (Graves, 1983, 1994). Furthermore, if children are to view themselves as authors and count themselves among those who write well and often, they need the support of a caring community of learners who will embrace the writer, as well as value the writing (Dudley-Marling, 1997).

These simple principles serve as the foundation for writing workshops, which can be opportunities for students to come together to learn, write, and share their work. While the writing workshop has transformed the face of elementary writing curricula, many teachers still struggle in their efforts to create genuine learning communities in which children engage in authentic forms of writing. As one veteran teacher with 12 years of writing workshop experience said:

I feel like all the right pieces are in place, but it never really comes together. I still always feel as if students write for an audience of one—me. I try to create a genuine writing community, but it always feels forced or contrived. Sometimes I wonder if it's even possible.

This teacher is not alone in her concerns and she raises important questions: Is it possible to create authentic writing communities among elementary students? If so, how do we go about doing this?

Joining the Writer's Club

Concerns such as these are what led Stephen Schroeder, a teacher education student at the University of Central Florida, to start up a Friday evening writer's club for elementary students. As a prospective teacher, he wanted children to view writing not as a required academic task, but rather as a powerful process that could enrich their lives. As a community leader, he hoped to spark the interest of children within the area. Schroeder envisioned a program in which interested participants could come together to celebrate writing. Reasoning that children would want to write if they were given an encouraging and creative context in which to do it, he decided to organize a community-based writer's club that would draw from the local area and operate separately from the school system.

His purpose in starting the writer's club was three-fold. First, he wanted to create a supportive and low-risk environment in which children's writing could be nurtured. Second, he wanted to establish a forum in which he could be a "writer's influence," a role model who enjoyed writing and valued it as a part of everyday life. And, finally, he wanted to help legitimize writing in the minds of the students with whom he worked. Knowing that

children's lives are often influenced by peer pressure and the urgency to engage in a whole range of activities, Schroeder hoped to position writing and participation in a thriving, literate community as a viable alternative to other, less healthful, choices.

• **Foundations.** *"If you build it they will come."* Although this bit of practical wisdom may have worked wonders in *Field of Dreams*, real life is another matter. From the beginning, Schroeder recognized that an authentic writing community could not simply be built and then imposed on the participants. If children were going to participate, they needed to play a role in constructing this community themselves; they needed to have a voice in shaping the community's identity and charting the group's course.

Schroeder began to solicit input from the children, gathering information on their thoughts about writing, as well as the kind of things they would like to see happen if a writer's group was formed. Although the majority of the respondents expressed negative attitudes about the writing they did in school, most were open to the possibility of being part of a writing community. While some children expressed vague enthusiasm, others offered concrete suggestions: the activities must be fun; participants should have a chance to do artwork as well as write; and the club should be made an official entity, complete with a special name, membership cards, elected officers, and regular rituals and activities. One child suggested that such a club would need money for supplies, and later returned with an empty soup can labeled simply, "Donations for Writer's Club." Responses such as these served as clear indications that young writers were capable of envisioning and charting a plan of action for the establishment of their own learning community.

• **Coming Together.** Working with the children, Schroeder organized a flexible framework for the inception of the writer's club. It was decided that the group would meet biweekly and focus on the dual processes of writing and illustration. Participants would come together to work towards the goals of writing, refining, and publishing their work. Meetings would include time for text development, as well as social interaction.

Six children, whose ages spanned the elementary grades, met in a neighborhood home for the initial gathering. The meeting began with the lighting of a "writing candle" and a brief discussion of the ways in which fire might symbolize writing. A "talking stick," borrowed from American Indian tradition, was used; each child added his or her thoughts as the stick was passed from person to person. Together, they named themselves the Crane Writer's Club (not only are cranes native to the area, the Red Crowned Crane is a symbol of "spirit" in Japan). The club received its official start as the members placed their "hands together in agreement and formed a fellowship of writers" (Schroeder, 1997).

In the weeks that followed, the participants brainstormed ideas, read children's books, and explored different modes of illustration. But most of all, they wrote. And they have been writing ever since. Some children have been eager and prolific authors, engaging easily and joyfully in the writing act. Others have needed a great deal of support simply to get past the obstacle of putting pencil to paper. Yet, all have been active members of the writing community, persevering in their writing until their pieces were ready for publication.

At a recent publication party, the children's final products were rich and varied. Some were short, others quite lengthy. Some pieces highlighted the written text, while others emphasized the visual aspects of publication, with much attention given to illustration. All of the final publications represented the work of engaged and active authors who took a great deal of pride in their work.

• **Making Strides.** The Crane Writer's Club has been up and running for a full year. The group currently meets for three hours on Friday evenings. The first two hours are devoted to writing, illustrating, and exploring different types of book design. The final hour is designated as a social time in which the children play organized games and have the opportunity to interact informally.

Members hail from a wide range of socioeconomic groups and represent a variety of cultural backgrounds. Approximately 75 percent of the participants are boys. Since the club's inception, membership has quadrupled, with new members joining at natural breaks in the club's schedule of projects and activities. Currently, a number of local children are waiting for their opportunity to join. This growth in membership necessitated a recent move out of family homes and into the local Boys and Girls Club building, which consequently engendered a whole new wave of interest.

In one short year, the Crane Writer's Club has blossomed into a genuine writing community, a place where elementary students voluntarily and eagerly participate in a full range of writing activities. The club provides a forum where young writers can take control of their own learning, collaborate with their peers, present their work to an audience, and develop leadership abilities.

Although still operated autonomously under Stephen Schroeder's leadership, the club is also a point of collaboration for children, parents, community leaders, and university faculty. Local high school and university students act as mentors and writing coaches for the group. Parent volunteers participate by providing snacks, donating supplies, and helping with logistics. Publication nights are open to families, friends, and interested others. Just as the club is becoming a community unto itself, it is also becoming an important fiber in the tapestry of the broader local community.

The Big Picture

Is it possible to create authentic writing communities among elementary students? The Crane Writer's Club project would indicate that the answer is an unequivocal "yes." As children engage in authentic writing experiences and participate fully in writing communities, they are capable of shaping these communities and developing a shared vision for influencing their social worlds (Dudley-Marling, 1997; Dyson, 1993; Shannon, 1995). After all, authentic learning communities are more than a group of students who happen to be engaged in the same activity. A genuine community is, as Sharon Murphy states, "the beginning of a shared focus, a shared purpose which eventually leads to a shared way of making sense of some aspect of the world" (Murphy, cited in Dudley-Marling, 1997, p. 3).

Certainly, logistical differences exist between mandatory classroom writing programs and after-school voluntary writing clubs. It seems that the potential exists, however, to find a good deal of common ground between the two. Quality writing programs, no matter where they are based, share a number of key elements. First, they are contextually appropriate. That is, they are programs that have been developed with a particular group of writers and their social context in mind. Second, they evolve. The program's structure is flexible enough that it can be adapted easily to meet the participants' needs, rather than requiring the participants to adapt to meet the needs of a static program. Finally, they are holistic. The programs are structured in such a way that writers have the opportunity to take part in the whole authoring process, with all its varied components. In the words of Nigel Hall, "If it is the experience of authorship which helps authors develop, then it follows that children should, from the start, be given opportunities to explore what it means to be an author" (Hall, 1989, p. ix). Where better to experience this than within the supportive framework of a writing community? It all starts with an invitation to join the writer's club.

References

Calkins, L. M. (1994). *The art of teaching writing* (2nd ed.). Portsmouth, NH: Heinemann.

Dudley-Marling, C. (1997). *Living with uncertainty: The messy reality of classroom practice.* Portsmouth, NH: Heinemann.

Dyson, A. H. (1993). *Social worlds of children: Learning to write in an urban primary school.* New York: Teachers College Press.

Graves, D. H. (1983). *Writing: Teachers and children at work.* Portsmouth, NH: Heinemann.

Graves, D. H. (1994). *A fresh look at writing.* Portsmouth, NH: Heinemann.

Hall, N. (1989). *Writing with reason.* London: Hodder & Stoughton.

Schroeder, S. (1997). *The writer's club: Teaching thinking to children.* Unpublished manuscript.

Shannon, P. (1995). *Texts, lies, and videotape.* Portsmouth, NH: Heinemann.

Short, K. G., Harste, J. C., & Burke, C. (1996). *Creating classrooms for authors and inquirers* (2nd ed.). Portsmouth, NH: Heinemann.

Chapter 12
Teacher Conferencing:
Let's Talk

Danese Collins,
Delaware Writing Project

Mrs. Collins: How's it going, Megan?

Megan: My writing, or the divorce?

Mrs. Collins: Are you writing about the divorce?

Megan: Well, I want to write a book to help other kids going through divorce, but I don't know where to start. It's pretty complicated. I understand how Dad feels, but I also understand how Mom feels. I love them both, so it's really hard for me to figure out where it all started.

Mrs. Collins: Are you thinking about starting your paper where the divorce started?

Megan: Well, yes, that would be the beginning, wouldn't it?

Mrs. Collins: Do you want me to know about the divorce, or do you want me to know how you feel about the divorce?

Megan: What I want is for you, plus all the kids in this class, plus any kids who might have to go through divorce, to know how I feel, and that if they have to go through it they can, because I've been there and I can help them.

Mrs. Collins: Megan, you really do have a lot to say about what is going on right now. Do you know some of the things you want to tell them?

Megan: Yes, I already know all of that.

Mrs. Collins: Well, Megan, do you think you could begin by saying some of what you just told me and then adding on those other things you want to say?

Megan: Yeah! Thanks, Mrs. Collins, that was a big help.

Mrs. Collins: Thank you, Megan. You have helped me understand how you are feeling, and that's very important to me.

When I walked away from Megan, I felt satisfied that she had a clear idea of where she was going next with her piece, and confident I had learned more about her. I also felt good because I knew Megan and I would talk soon about the fact that all writing does not necessarily have to be presented in a sequential order. A topic for a mini-lesson had evolved from our conversation. Certainly, the conversation fit well within the parameters set by Spandel and Stiggins (1996), when they described a writing conference as:

any one-on-one discussion between student and teacher (or between the student and any other trusted listener or writing coach). It tends to make the student writer feel special, and this, more than what is said, is the special contribution that the conference makes to writing instruction. The purpose of a conference is to help the student regroup, solve writing problems, plan for next steps, and, sometimes, see his or her writing from a slightly different perspective. A student should come away from a conference with an idea of where to go next or, at the very least, a clear sense of a useful writing question to answer. (p. 281)

More and more, I appreciate the power of writing conferences. Whether a conference takes place at the beginning, when ideas are being generated, or near the end of the process, when students are editing and moving their piece towards conventional writing, the conference has the potential to play a dynamic role. At any point in the writing process, the purposes of the conference are the same: to help young writers express themselves more clearly and to support them in developing their identities as writers.

Carol Avery (1993) asserts that most conferences result when the student needs help, when he or she is "stuck" in some way or another. The questions asked, and the responses given, permit the teacher/listener to gain important insights and knowledge about the writer and his or her piece of work. Lucy Calkins (1994) says the attentive listening of the teacher creates a magnetic force between the writer and the listener. If we think back to the conversation between Megan and me, it becomes evident that the easy conversational flow allowed me to gain some important insights and knowledge about Megan in only a few minutes. As I walked away, I was much more knowledgeable about her history, and I knew Megan felt confident and ready to begin her writing.

Nancie Atwell (1998) tells about attending a writing conference in which the speaker informed the audience that conferencing was really about revising. She was quick to refute such a notion by saying that a conference is not about one particular point of the writing process, but rather it is appropriate for a variety of purposes depending upon the needs of the student and teacher. Calkins (1994) agrees, explaining that she arbitrarily divides conferences into categories that are primarily based on the purpose of the conference:

Content (focuses on content, subject, or topic)
Design (focuses on genre or format)
Process (focuses on what writers do when they write)
Evaluation (focuses on child's analysis and evaluation of a writing piece)
Editorial (focuses on editing and the conventions of print)

Not every writer will require a conference in each of these areas. The lines of separation are not always obvious, either; sometimes, several obstacles can be overcome within one session. For example, by opening Megan's conference with a general question, rather than one aimed directly at her writing, we were able to proceed through questions of both content and design. When we concluded, she knew how to begin her piece and had ideas about what she wanted to include. She also had a clear vision about form, knowing that she wanted to design a small book to help other children who might be experiencing a similar problem. Fortunately for Megan, we conferred when she needed it and she was able to continue writing. Had I made Megan wait for a conference until she completed her whole draft, she may have changed topics out of frustration or written a very boring story with too many details.

This was not Megan's first writing for the school year. Previously, she had penned many pieces and we had had many short conferences. Spandel and Stiggins (1996) prefer short conferences, noting that some of the most effective conferences occur on the run. Short conferences also enable the teacher to reach more children. By staggering conferences and questions throughout the writing process, the student is able to concentrate on the one task or question at hand, rather than trying to remember a multitude of questions for a delayed conference and then applying several responses that may become confusing.

One of the goals of conferencing is to help writers begin to internalize the type of questioning that takes place so that they can ultimately confer with themselves. By asking certain questions repetitively, the teacher acts as a model for such reflection and helps the student see a pattern of what type of questions to ask himself or herself. Through self-conferencing, the writer takes another step toward independence, and toward ownership over the writing. In Megan's case, she was able to do this and dive into her writing after getting initial support from the teacher.

At our final conference, I decided to take a slightly different approach. Megan's paper seemed to be in good shape, containing only one spelling error. I asked her if there was anything in particular she would like us to look at together. Her immediate response was for us to look at the word "embearased." She knew she had misspelled it. We next looked at her piece together and celebrated each of the difficult words she had successfully spelled on her own. We also celebrated her fine sense of when to use capitalization, as well as her excellent use of punctuation marks.

Next, we talked about layout. Megan asked if she could use a bookmaking program on our computer. She was moving the following week, and it was extremely important to her that she make two copies of the book before leaving. She wanted to leave one copy in our school library and the other one in our classroom library. Eventually, she made five copies, extending her intended audience to Mom, Dad, and Oprah. When her work was completed, she shared it with her classmates. We celebrated the wonderful job she

had done sharing her feelings and inviting others to know that it is okay to have such feelings.

Teacher conferencing provides a wonderful opportunity for both the writer and the teacher. Although it may sound trite, conferencing truly does provide the wind beneath the wings of countless writing students who are able to soar to heights we teachers never dared. Why? Because we take great pleasure in celebrating their successes as we provide those thoughtful, purposeful conversations called teacher conferencing.

References

Atwell, N. (1998). *In the middle: New understandings about writing, reading, and learning* (2nd ed.). Portsmouth, NH: Boynton/Cook-Heinemann.

Avery, C. (1993). *And with a light touch.* Portsmouth, NH: Heinemann.

Calkins, L. M. (1994). *The art of teaching writing* (2nd ed.). Portsmouth, NH: Heinemann.

Spandel, V., & Stiggins, R. (1996). *Creating writers: Linking writing assessment and instruction.* New York: Longman.

Content Connections

Chapter 13
Math Moments

Sandra Atkins,
INSIGHT Professional Development,
Wright Group/McGraw-Hill

Jill Perry,
Rowan University

The 1st-graders and I sit in a circle on the floor. On a sheet of paper, I've drawn a circle that is divided into two unequal pieces. On each piece, I've written "1/2." I ask the children what they think about the drawing. I get no response. Then, I ask them to pretend the drawn circle is a cake or pizza, and ask what they think about how it was sliced. A silent group of children looks back; not one child makes a comment. I cut the paper along the drawn lines. I give the smaller section to one child and the larger section to another. I ask what they think about my sharing "cake" or "pizza" in this way. No one replies. I begin cutting those initial pieces into smaller unequal "slices." I give these slices to other children in the class. Periodically, I stop and ask the children what they think. Still, not one child says a word. They just sit quietly and watch as I continue cutting the pieces into smaller pieces until each child in the room has a piece of our "cake" or "pizza." Some of the "slices" are quite large; others are pitiful little slivers. I ask the children one last time what they think about these "slices," saying, "How would you feel if this were a real cake and I gave out slices like this?" Finally, one child says, "Mrs. Hughes says it's better to have something than nothing and you should be happy you have anything at all."

Mrs. Hughes had asked me to teach an introductory fraction lesson to her 1st-graders. She was interested in observing the questioning techniques I use and listening to the responses her students would give. In planning this lesson, I considered the students' likely non-school experiences of equal shares. I thought that using a food scenario would ensure a wonderful discussion about fair shares and equal parts. I decided that I would use unequal shares to get the conversation started, and planned to introduce the term "one-half" and the idea that halves from the same whole should be equal. I did not anticipate the strong influence of Mrs. Hughes's philosophy. I had to agree, however, that it *is* better to have something than nothing, and I was happy to have an explanation for the failure of my lesson.

Math moments occur when children are actively engaged in meaningful mathematical investigations. They begin to act as mathematicians by offering conjectures, defending their conjectures, and refuting each other's conjectures by offering counterexamples (Banchoff, 2000; Hersh, 1997; Lakatos, 1976; Popper, 1963/2002). Meaningful mathematical conversations are not filtered through the teacher (Atkins, 1999; Corwin, 1996). Math moments are the times in which unanticipated mathematical connections are made—the surprises, the discoveries, and the wondering. In the above lesson, I found that what I thought would facilitate a wonderful mathematical discussion about equal shares actually revealed the management techniques used in the classroom.

The National Council of Teachers of Mathematics (NCTM) (1989, 1991, 2000) suggests using a multidimensional approach to planning and teaching that considers both content and process. They also describe the processes that should be used in teaching and learning mathematics (e.g., problem solving, communication, reasoning and proof, connections, and representation) (NCTM, 2000). This type of planning helps us to create mathematical moments in which children actively explore and communicate mathematically (orally, in writing, and pictorially). It is during such mathematical moments that we are able to glimpse our students' understandings and misunderstandings. Although there is no guarantee of lesson success, by planning for math moments we can learn about students' conceptual understandings, further develop these understandings, and learn about the connections they are making to other content areas; I even learned about classroom social "rules."

Planning for math moments is different from planning a more traditional lesson. In planning for math moments, we:

- Determine the underlying mathematical concepts to be learned, not just the procedures or skills
- Consider the children's possible non-school and prior school experiences
- Plan to find out what the students already know and be prepared to change directions
- Plan to extend wait time, ask for multiple solution methods, and have students defend their answers (whether or not they are correct)
- Choose an appropriate task (What problem solving will they do? How will they be reasoning mathematically? How will they communicate their reasoning to you and their peers?)
- Consider the materials that may be used during the lesson, how they will be used, and when the children will have access to the materials.

Determining the Underlying Mathematical Concepts

Mathematics curriculum documents are full of the topics and skills that children should know and be able to do. The focus is on the task and the topic to be explored. Children should know how to add,

subtract, multiply, and divide. They should be able to find the area of a region, work with fractional parts, and measure a multitude of objects using a variety of measurement tools. To teach and evaluate students on these tasks, however, it is critical to know the underlying math concepts. If a child really understands the concept of area, what is it that he or she understands? Some of the underlying conceptual understandings related to area are that area is measured in square units and there is a "best fit" square unit that can be used to measure regions based on the size of the region (e.g., square millimeters, square inches, square yards, square kilometers, square miles). In planning for math moments, we shift our focus to the concepts to be developed and the experiences that will most likely facilitate this conceptual development.

Building on Possible Non-School and Prior School Experiences

In a traditional mathematics setting, the focus of the lessons is often on learning procedures and memorizing rules. We tend to make assumptions about what the children know and do not know. Instructional decisions often are based on the order and presentation of material in a textbook. We tend to forget about children's prior school and non-school mathematical experiences. If we do not find out what our students know and do not know, however, we waste a great deal of time. In planning for math moments, we consider our students' prior experiences and plan to find out what they do know (Baroody & Standifer, 1993).

Find Out What They Already Know and Be Prepared To Change Directions

The importance of determining students' prior understandings became very evident when teaching a lesson on money to a group of 4th-graders. According to the lesson outline, we were to begin by identifying the different pieces of currency, shift to discussing ways to make equivalent dollar amounts, and end with the students engaging in an activity. I began by asking the students to tell me everything they knew about money. I found out that they could identify all of the different coins and paper currency and even provide suggestions for helping younger children make the distinctions (e.g. pennies are brown; dimes are the smallest; it says "one cent" on the penny and "five cents" on the nickel). They knew equivalencies of dollar and cent amounts. For example, they could tell me that six dimes or two quarters and a dime or 12 nickels are all equivalent. Then, they began telling me about tax on purchases. Instead of doing the planned activity, which would have been a review of concepts they already knew, we began determining the tax on different purchase amounts. We spent the majority of class time building on the students' prior experiences instead of repeating what they already knew. (It is important to remember that I would not expect all 4th-graders to have the same understandings as this particular group.) Therefore, in planning for mathematical moments, we need to plan time to find out what the students know and then be willing and prepared to change directions in response to that knowledge.

Extend Wait Time and Ask for Alternative Solution Methods

Traditionally, the pace in the mathematics classroom has been very fast. The teacher asks a question and then calls on students until a correct answer is given. Then, a new question is asked. Throughout this question and answer time, students are encouraged for trying and praised for giving the correct answer. Very rarely are students asked to describe their reasoning or give alternative methods for finding the answers.

In teaching for mathematical moments, we slow down the pace of the lesson. We ask students to share and defend the methods they use to solve a problem, whether or not their answers are correct. We also encourage students to share multiple strategies for solving a problem. When only one method is shared and validated by the teacher, some students believe that the shared method is the only way to solve the problem. It is important that children understand that more than one method for solving problems can be mathematically correct.

In the elementary mathematics classroom, we want children to become proficient at solving

computation problems. Rather than building proficiency solely from memorizing math facts and procedures, we design lessons that develop conceptual understandings of number and the operations (number sense). A wonderful number sense activity is Dutch Squares or Math Squares (G. H. Wheatley, personal communication, February 26, 1997). In one version of the activity, four numbers are placed in a two by two grid (see Figure 1). Students are asked to find the total for the four boxes. This is to be done without paper and pencil or a calculator.

The following is an example of a Math Square problem that I used with 3rd- and 4th-graders.

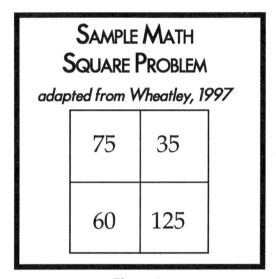

Figure 1

After displaying the problem on the board or overhead, I ask the students to raise their hands when they know the answer. I then wait for all or almost all of the students to raise their hands because I want them to understand that this is a thinking activity and not a speed activity. After the majority of the students have raised their hands, I tell them that I do not want them to tell me the answer; instead, I ask them to tell me how they got the answer. Often, many of the hands go down. I then give them some additional time to think of a way to explain their thinking; again, I wait for a majority of the students to raise their hands. After each response I ask if any of the students had solved the problem in a different way. Consequently, the students and I heard four different ways of interpreting and solving this problem. The following are examples of methods students have used to solve the problem.

Method 1:
Chas: I added the four numbers up.
Teacher: How did you add them up? Where did you start?
Chas: I added the 75 and the 35 and that was 110.
Teacher: How did you get 110?
Chas: I added 5 and 5 and got 10. And then I put the one over there (pointing in the air to the left) and 7 and 3 and 1 is 11 so 110.
Teacher: Okay.
Chas: Then I added 125 to that, and 60 to that.
Teacher: What did you get when you added 125?
Chas: 235.
Teacher: And when you added 60?
Chas: 295.

Method 2:
Emily: I added the 75 and 60 first.
Teacher: What did you get?
Emily: 135
Teacher: How did you get 135?
Emily: I added 70 and 60 and got 130 and then 5 more is 135.
Teacher: Then what did you do?
Emily: Then I added 125 and that's 260, plus 35 is 295.
Teacher: How did you get 260?
Emily: 100 and 100 is 200. 35 and 5 is 40 and 20 more is 60, so 260.
Teacher: And then what did you do?
Emily: I added the 35 and got 295.

Method 3:
Jodi: I added the 75 and the 125 first.
Teacher: What did you get?
Jodi: 200.
Teacher: How did you get 200?
Jodi: 75 and 25 is 100 and 100 more is 200.
Teacher: Okay.
Jodi: Then I added 35 and 60 and got 95 so 295.

Method 4:
Jaime: I got 67,660.
Teacher: How did you get 67,660?
Jaime: I added 7,535 and 60,125.
Teacher: Oh, I see...

Chas worked clockwise, using a traditional algorithm. Emily worked counterclockwise, adding left to right and breaking numbers apart to make tens. That is,

25 is 20 and 5
$35 + 5 = 40$
40 plus the additional 20 is 60

Jodi added the 75 and 125 first, making 200. She then added the 60 and 35 together and then combined the resulting 95 with the 200. Finally, Jaime did not see the grid as four separate numbers, but rather as two multi-digit numbers written in boxes. Consequently, he added 7,535 and 60,125, instead of adding 75, 35, 60, and 125. Had I not asked for multiple solution methods I would not have known about Jaime's confusion concerning the task itself, nor would Jaime have understood why his answer was so different from those of the other students.

Notice that in the above task each of the children was asked to describe his or her method for finding the answer at each step in the process, even if it was apparent to the teacher what the student had done and that it was correct or incorrect. In this way, all of the students in the class were able to hear alternative strategies for solving the problem. This also provided the children with an opportunity to describe their thinking and develop their mathematical language. The questioning in this process was as simple as, "How do you know?" and "How did you get that?"

Choosing the Task
The choosing of an appropriate task is key to facilitating mathematical moments in the classroom. A task may be as simple as a good problem or may be a more elaborate investigation. The key is that the lesson or the problem reflects the

conceptual understanding to be gained. At first glance, the Math Squares activity gives students practice with adding double-digit numbers. However, it also gives them an opportunity to work with the underlying concepts of number and addition. That is, numbers can be broken apart and put back together in several different ways to obtain the same amount (decomposing and composing numbers); and the order in which numbers are combined can be changed and still give the same result (commutativity).

The Use of Manipulative Materials

Planning for math moments includes considering the timing and use of manipulative materials, the structuring of groups, and the distribution of materials. Research shows that students begin building conceptual understandings through experiences with appropriate concrete materials before developing more abstract understandings (Baroody & Standifer, 1993; Carpenter, Fennema, Franke, Levi, & Empson, 1999; Crowley, 1987). The goal is for the student eventually to move away from dependence on a manipulative material and instead use symbolic representations. We tend to give children manipulative materials that we feel are appropriate for completing a task. Whether they need the manipulative materials or not, children often will use the materials simply because they are on the table. In preparing for math moments, we want to make manipulative materials available, but not impose their use.

Conclusion

While we cannot script math moments, we can plan for them. By focusing on conceptual understandings, increasing wait time, encouraging multiple explanations, and building mathematical experiences from students' understandings rather than from the planned activity, math moments are more likely to occur. Math moments occur as a result of a teacher's willingness to question and listen to his or her students. They hinge on a

teacher's wanting to know what his or her students are thinking and what sense they are making of the mathematics. Lessons that focus on concepts rather than broad topics or specific procedures and skills allow us to optimize our class time by building on children's conceptual understandings, rather than reviewing the mathematics they already know. Math moments fill a mathematics classroom with surprises, discoveries, and wondering.

References

Atkins, S. L. (1999). Listening to students: The power of mathematical conversations. *Teaching Children Mathematics, 5,* 289-295.

Banchoff, T. F. (2000). The mathematician as a child and children as mathematicians. *Teaching Children Mathematics, 6,* 350-356.

Baroody, A. J., & Standifer, D. J. (1993). Addition and subtraction in the primary grades. In R. J. Jensen (Ed.), *Research ideas for the classroom: Early childhood mathematics* (pp. 72-102). New York: Macmillan.

Carpenter, T. P., Fennema, E., Franke, M. L., Levi, L., & Empson, S. B. (1999). *Children's mathematics: Cognitively guided instruction.* Portsmouth, NH: Heinemann.

Corwin, R. B. (1996). Supporting classroom talk. In *Talking mathematics: Supporting children's voices.* Portsmouth, NH: Heinemann.

Crowley, M. L. (1987). The Van Hiele model of the development of geometric thought. In M. M. Lindquist & A. P. Shulte (Eds.), *Learning and teaching geometry, K-12* (pp. 1-16). Reston, VA: National Council of Teachers of Mathematics.

Hersh, R. (1997). *What is mathematics, really?* New York: Oxford University Press.

Lakatos, I. (1976). *Proof and refutations: The logic of mathematical discovery.* Cambridge: Cambridge University Press.

Popper, K. R. (2002). *Conjectures and refutations: The growth of scientific knowledge.* London: Routledge. (Original work published 1963)

National Council of Teachers of Mathematics. (1989). *Curriculum and evaluation of standards for school mathematics.* Reston, VA: Author.

National Council of Teachers of Mathematics. (1991). *Professional standards for school mathematics.* Reston, VA: Author.

National Council of Teachers of Mathematics. (2000). *Principles and standards for school mathematics.* Reston, VA: Author.

Chapter 14
Inquiring Minds Want To Know:
Inquiry Science in the Elementary Classroom

Deirdre Englehart,
University of Central Florida

"Mommy, where did this pine cone come from?"
"Does Frank [our class rabbit] see in color or black and white?"
"Can I use magnets to make a compass?"
"What can rocks be used for?"

My reply to each of these inquiries:
"That's a great question—I wonder how we can find out."

I am a teacher. I teach my own children, elementary students, college students, and other educators. At every level, students have questions. Curiosity is a natural human characteristic. When we give students the freedom to pursue their curiosity and the tools to explore, we involve them in inquiry. By doing so, we give students the opportunity to learn about their world and construct knowledge; through such learning and construction, they become better citizens of the Earth. But what does inquiry look like in a class-room? How does it compare to "hands-on" science? How do we assess inquiry? Why should we use inquiry methods to teach science? These are all valid questions worthy of exploration.

How Does Inquiry Compare to "Hands-on" Science?

Science teaching has steadily progressed from a traditional approach towards more hands-on learning, and finally towards promoting the higher level thinking and habits of mind that are the trademark of the inquiry process. A traditional approach relies heavily on textbooks as the source of information about scientific facts. Usually, students are seated and read facts from a text; later, they are tested on their recall of those facts.

Hands-on science is a great step forward in science education. Students learn scientific concepts by actively manipulating materials. The lesson is outlined for the teacher with specific goals and activities that are followed in a cookbook fashion. Students are actively involved in manipulating materials, but they see the teacher as the source of information. Teachers and students enjoy the involvement of hands-on activities. Teachers also like the format of the activities, which can be planned for a specific amount of time, and with all students involved in the same activity.

In inquiry, students use process skills as a guide to explore and investigate scientific concepts. They are the "scientists" manipulating materials in order to discover scientific knowledge. The teacher does not know the end result of the inquiry process. Students are actively involved in the lesson, but the direction they take in their inquiry is not predetermined. Inquiry is based upon the students' questions and interests. Students develop questions and try to discover answers through investigation and research. They take their investigations in directions that are meaningful to them. The teacher's role becomes that of a facilitator, not as the "keeper of knowledge."

While hands-on science and inquiry are both valuable approaches, there is a definitive difference in the thinking that occurs when students are involved in inquiry versus hands-on activities. Inquiry is a step above hands-on science in that students use thinking processes and problem solving when they question, develop investigations to answer their questions, and analyze the results. Hands-on activities, such as science kits, can be used as a preliminary step of inquiry to promote a base of knowledge before students pursue their own questions.

What Is Inquiry?

In the publication *National Science Education Standards* the authors state,

Students at all grade levels and in every domain of science should have the opportunity to use scientific inquiry and develop the ability to think and act in ways associated with inquiry, including asking questions, planning and conducting investigations, using appropriate tools and techniques to gather data, think critically and logically about relationships between evidence and explanations, constructing and analyzing alternative explanations, and communicating scientific arguments. (National Research Council, 1996, p. 105)

Although this statement sounds rather complicated, experience shows that children are natural inquirers. From a very early age, children practice inquiry as a way of finding out about the world around them. Children use their natural curiosity to guide them as they observe their surroundings and use their senses. They make predictions and repeatedly experiment with objects to find out how they work and what they do. Children then connect this knowledge with previous experiences

to build understanding. Elementary students have this same curiosity. As teachers, we can guide students to continue their explorations and foster their sense of inquiry and wonder about the world.

What Does Inquiry Look Like in a Classroom?

While we know that all inquiry should be based upon questions that students actively investigate, inquiry can take different forms. Although there is not one specific formula for students to follow, process skills are a natural guide. "When learners interact with the world in a scientific way, they find themselves observing, questioning, hypothesizing, predicting, investigating, interpreting, and communicating. . . . Process skills play a critical role in helping children develop scientific ideas" (National Science Foundation, p. 52). Process skills are closely linked with the inquiry process because they provide avenues through which students can gather and interpret information. By teaching these process skills, we provide students with the tools of inquiry. Process skills can be used in any order, can be repeated, and are used throughout an investigation. The first five skills concern information gathering and the last five refer directly to the inquiry process (see Figure 1).

Students who have little or no experience with inquiry may need more structure as they work through the process. With practice, they will become more adept at asking good questions and following through with investigations and conclusions. The inquiry approach can be appropriately described as a progression through levels of inquiry. "The degree to which teachers structure what students do is sometimes referred to as 'guided' versus 'open' inquiry" (National Research Council, 2000, p. 29).

Teachers can assess the students' comfort level in particular areas, as well as their overall comfort level with the inquiry process, to determine an appropriate level of inquiry. By providing "structured-activity inquiry periods," teachers can observe students interacting with materials and begin to establish the patterns for inquiry in the classroom (Pearce, 1999, p. 28). It is then valuable to work with students to evaluate their questions and begin to develop the ability to ask good questions—questions that can be easily investigated.

Through guidance at the beginning level of inquiry, teachers can help students better understand the overall process. Students and teachers can work together to lay the foundation of inquiry and model appropriate activities. Then, students can progress through the different levels, depending on their comfort level with the science content and processes. Students should move through the stages of inquiry towards greater independence. They should take on more responsibility for the questions and become more independent in their investigations. The following describes four different levels of inquiry:

• **Guided Exploration.** In guided exploration, the teacher designs a question or questions for the

---

SCIENCE PROCESS SKILLS

Observing—	Students use one or more of their senses to gather information about an object or an event. Students should be given experiences to help them refine their observational skills and focus on what is directly observed.
Predicting—	Students make an educated guess about future events, based upon their previous knowledge and observations.
Classifying—	Students use observations to group objects or events into categories based upon properties.
Communicating—	Students use words, graphs, and other representations to share and receive information.
Measuring—	Typically, students estimate the measurements of an object. They then use standard and nonstandard units to gather information about an object (e.g., length, mass, and time).
Formulating Hypotheses—	Students state what they expect will happen in an experiment.
Controlling Variables—	Specific variables may affect the outcome of an experiment. Students should be able to identify variables that may affect the outcome and keep them constant while manipulating only the independent variable.
Defining Operationally—	Students take their observations and think about them, then write a definition of what an object does.
Interpreting Data—	Students collect data through their observations and other process skills, organize the data, and draw conclusions.
Investigating—	Investigating incorporates numerous process skills. Students observe, gather information, formulate a hypothesis, and develop an experiment to answer a question. As they do this, they work to make sure the test is fair and they control different variables. Then, they interpret the results of their experiment and communicate them.

Figure 1

students to pursue. The teacher also develops activities to support the questions. While students are involved in hands-on activities, the activities are mostly teacher-directed. Guided explorations can be a beneficial starting point for teachers to use in modeling the inquiry process. The teacher can focus on one or more process skills throughout the investigation.

• **Foundational Inquiry.** At the foundational inquiry level, the teacher provides a series of activities that invite student participation. The activities will help students develop a base of knowledge. After participation in the activities, students then generate questions and begin their inquiries. At this level, students who do not have previous knowledge or experiences develop a foundation of understanding through the activities before they initiate their own questions. This level is valuable for teachers who have science kits and activities, as these activities can be used as a base for the inquiry element that follows.

• **Observational Inquiry.** Many times, it is appropriate for students to observe different items. The science center/area in the classroom should have many interesting items available that could generate student interest. Exploration of these materials becomes the starting point for students' investigations. At this level, students become familiar with different materials and develop a base of knowledge that can lead to inquiry. Once the students have made observations, they begin to form their questions and develop investigations based upon the observations.

• **Open Inquiry.** In open inquiry, students develop their own questions that may or may not be related to class activities or studies. Once students are given the opportunity to ask questions and investigate over a period of time, they will continue to open their minds to experiences that may lead to questions. To facilitate personal inquiry in the classroom, an "I Wonder" chart posted in the classroom is recommended. Students can use this chart to record questions as they think of them. The teacher then can discuss questions and procedures to help students develop their inquiry.

How Do We Create a Learning Environment That Promotes Inquiry?

"Inquiry-based teaching requires careful attention to creating learning environments and experiences

LEVELS OF INQUIRY

	Guided Exploration	Foundational Explorations	Observational Inquiry	Open Inquiry
Role of the Teacher	Teacher designs activities and experiments for students to follow.	Teacher provides activities to create foundation of information.	Teacher presents interesting items for students to observe.	Teacher helps students in the inquiry process as a facilitator.
Role of the Student	Students follow directions set forth by teacher in order to answer a question.	Students develop questions after they have participated in a series of activities.	Students develop questions based on observations of materials.	Students think of questions based on their own experiences.
Level of Inquiry	Beginning level of inquiry.	Moderate level of inquiry.	Moderate level of inquiry.	High level of inquiry.

Figure 2

where students can confront new ideas, deepen their understandings, and learn to think logically and critically about the world around them" (National Research Council, 2000, p. 73). As teachers, we create the climate in the classroom. One of the most important aspects of the learning environment is establishing a community of learners. One way we can do this is by modeling respectful interactions for our students. We also encourage students to interact in positive ways and to develop relationships. By providing students with social skills, we help them work together and connect to each other in positive ways. Children must know that they are in a safe environment—a place where they are free to explore and make mistakes without fear of humiliation. Students need opportunities to act independently and responsibly in their environment. We want students to feel accepted and to know that we value their contributions.

As teachers, we become models of inquiry. Children learn more from what we do than from what we say. Inquiry thus gives teachers a wonderful opportunity to promote a sense of curiosity and wonder. When we share our own interests and pursue them with children, we are again modeling the significance and value we place on inquiry.

We can foster students' curiosity by making various materials available. Through their experiences with these objects students begin to make observations, think scientifically, and build conclusions. It is essential to have adequate materials available for all students to manipulate and explore. Begin by identifying a specific place in the room as a "Science Center" and stock it with a general selection of science items, such as:

rocks	feathers	magnets
kaleidoscope	leaves	seeds
mirrors	flashlights	shells
prisms	colored lenses	binoculars
stethoscope	microscope	tornado tube
periscope	wire	classroom pets
plants	soil	light bulbs
batteries	musical instruments	

When beginning a particular content area, teachers can add relevant items to the center.

How and What Should Be Assessed Through the Inquiry Process?

The National Science Education Standards suggest that students should be assessed in three learning outcomes of inquiry-based teaching: conceptual understandings in science, abilities to perform scientific inquiry, and understandings about inquiry (National Research Council, 1996). Through a multitude of assessments, we gain a clear picture of what our students have learned conceptually, how they use and understand inquiry, and the overall progress they have made in a particular area. When assessing inquiry, it is most important to look beyond factual memorization. Students should have opportunities to demonstrate what they have learned. Some of the following assessment methods are valuable devices for teachers committed to a philosophy that honors inquiry:

- **Observations.** Observations occur naturally in the classroom as the teacher circulates and watches children interact with materials and other students. It is important to record observations and anecdotal comments in order to keep track of student progress in a systematic and organized way.
- **Conferences.** Teachers can meet regularly with students to discuss progress in an interview format. These one-on-one sessions assure the teacher that each student has learned the concepts being taught.
- **Portfolios.** Portfolios are a collection of a student's work over a period of time. They may include projects, journal entries, graphs, illustrations, etc. By sharing their portfolios in a conference format, students can demonstrate what they have learned.
- **Performance Assessments.** Performance assessments require students to synthesize and apply concepts they have gained through classroom experiences. They demonstrate students' abilities to perform certain skills and tasks.
- **Self-Evaluation.** Self-evaluation gives students time to focus on their growth and to set goals for themselves. Self-evaluation may include surveys, checklists, and discussions.

Why Use Inquiry in the Classroom?

When we use inquiry we inspire learning for all the children in our classrooms and we teach them how to learn. Inquiry is a process and a tool, not an end in itself. In our ever-changing world, students will encounter scientific phenomena and be expected to respond to it. Teachers must strive to help them develop the ability to gather information, investigate an idea, analyze data, and then use the information. By using inquiry, we help students construct their own knowledge; even more important, we provide them with the tools to access and gather information so that the process of constructing knowledge becomes a natural function of life.

References and Resources

Doris, E. (1991). *Doing what scientists do: Children learn to investigate their world.* Portsmouth, NH: Heinemann.

Moscovici, H., & Nelson, T. H. (1998). Shifting from activity mania to inquiry. *Science and Children, 35*(4), 14-17, 40.

National Research Council. (1996). *National science education standards.* Washington, DC: National Academy Press.

National Research Council. (2000). *Inquiry and the National Science Education Standards.* Washington, DC: National Academy Press.

National Science Foundation. (n.d.). *Foundations monograph: Inquiry: Thoughts, views, and strategies for the K-5 classroom.* Arlington, VA: National Science Foundation.

Pearce, C. R. (1999). *Nurturing inquiry: Real science for the elementary classroom.* Portsmouth, NH: Heinemann.

Saul, W., Reardon, J., Schmidt, A., Pearce, C., Blackwood, D., & Bird, M. D. (1993). *Science workshop: A whole language approach.* Portsmouth, NH: Heinemann.

Chapter 15
Using Projects To Inquire About Social Studies in 2nd Grade

Jeanette Allison,
College of the Sequoias

"We don't have time for social studies anymore. All the district wants is high reading scores. These children know how to decode words, but few can use those words in real life. Why can't children explore their real world and learn the basics at the same time?"

This comment represents a sentiment common to many teachers: The best way children learn "the basics" is through direct inquiry about their world. As their world is a *social* world, their inquiry should include social studies.

Inquiry learning is an effective method to help children learn about social studies directly. Inquiry learning varies in the type of inquiry, who leads the inquiry, and the approach for using inquiry (Hartman, 1993) (see Figure 1). The project approach is highlighted in the "Approaches Using Inquiry" section of Figure 1 because I consider it the most desirable method of inquiry.

What Is the Project Approach?
The project approach uses in-depth research studies—or projects—as the main tool for inquiry. Ideally, the project approach involves *guided inquiry*, which means that both children and teachers lead the learning. There also is a balance between child-generated and teacher-directed learning, with children's interests and questions heavily influencing the curriculum. Projects provide children with real-world environments in which to learn about social studies. Typically, the children choose or vote for project topics (Allison, 1999; Helm & Katz, 2001).

How Are Projects Implemented?
Teachers need to understand two main things about implementing projects. First, a lot of "pre-project" groundwork must be done. The pre-project time is useful, also, for establishing children's and adults' roles. Second, a project usually progresses through three main phases.

Before engaging in a large project, I recommend practicing first with "tabletop" projects. These are small projects children can plan and create at their tables (e.g., making a favorite animal). This allows them to learn the basic steps of project work, and discover how to connect projects to content areas such as social studies.

The teacher's role is to guide children through planning, preparing, constructing, and sharing tabletop projects in the same manner they will use for a larger project. Constructions can occur on the floor, on the sidewalk, or in the hall. Once children grasp the project approach, the teacher can begin eliciting ideas for a larger project. These ideas then are sifted to identify a larger project topic.

Topics are selected from children's lives—their experiences and interests. Social studies topics are simple to choose because they involve children's everyday lives. Here are some tips for choosing relevant topics:

• Be sure children can directly investigate real environments and people (e.g., school cafeteria). Don't expect them to imagine "being there" in their minds (e.g., "Okay kids, picture in your mind a trip to the rain forest..."). It must be possible for them to be "there."

• Be sure children can revisit people and places directly connected to the project (e.g., a follow-up interview with a school cafeteria employee).

• Choose topics children can relate to easily and find resources about, such as: homes, shelters, pets, gardens, toy factory, ice cream factory, dairy, school buildings, neighborhood businesses, hospital, police station, and so on.

Phases and Time Frames

Projects typically go through three main inquiry phases. Not all children will be involved to an equal degree at the same time. Some children will participate during the entire project; others will dabble in the project at different stages. Keep in mind that project work makes up some, but not all, of the curriculum. However, I prefer project work to be a focal point in the curriculum.

Phase one: Getting started/Creating a focus. The beginning of any project is the most time-consuming. This phase includes assessing children's interests and backgrounds, deciding on a topic, brainstorming possible next steps, gathering resources, identifying social studies resources, and assigning initial responsibilities and roles. The teacher's role is to continually write down children's ideas in order to model connections between the ideas, written language, and social studies concepts. At this point, creating a common focus is very important to the project's outcome. Semantic maps (webs) are very useful in developing common foci.

• *Using K-W-L to create foci.* Another useful strategy to help children focus their inquiry is K-W-L (What Children **Know**; What Children **Want** To Know; What Children **Learned**). Once a topic has been chosen, find out what children know and what they want to learn with the project. Many K-W-Ls need to be developed throughout the entire project, because many foci will emerge from the children's inquiries. Check K-W-Ls against the concepts and standards on which the project is

INQUIRY LEARNING CONTINUUM

Type of Inquiry	Who Leads the Inquiry	Approaches Using Inquiry
Pure Inquiry	Children: Child-directed learning	Free Play Open Discovery Learning
Guided Inquiry (recommended)	Children and Teacher: Balance between child-generated and teacher-directed learning	**PROJECT APPROACH** Child-Generated Investigations Reggio Emilia
Directed Inquiry	Teacher: Teacher- and commercial-curriculum directed learning	Thematic Units Scientific Inquiry

Figure 1

based (see Shelters Project later in this chapter).

• *Gathering resources.* Collect resources ahead of time, if possible. The children themselves can contribute some resources. Standard resources include: all types of odds and ends; toilet paper and paper towel rolls; all sizes of boxes; craft items (e.g., ribbons, buttons, fabric, glitter); plastic containers; empty cardboard egg cartons; milk cartons; masking tape; glue; and so on. Contact people and organizations in the community for potential field trips and guest speakers.

• *Building background knowledge.* Effective inquiry during project work depends on background knowledge that the children share. Sometimes, children already have this common knowledge (e.g., they talk to the mail carrier every day at school); other times, the teacher and children create this knowledge together (e.g., visiting a pet store, then building a project from that visit). Often, background knowledge begins with a "starter" event. Knowledge gained from this event is expressed in personal journals, semantic maps, lists, drawings, and discussion groups.

Phase two: Project in full action. By the second phase, the project gains momentum. Many children will have experimented with project ideas, plans, vocabulary, and basic skills through initial research, events, constructions, writings, and role-playing. Phase two is the messiest and noisiest part of the project. Do not panic; this is good news because it means the children are energized and motivated by their inquiry. They will be very productive if given teacher support and simple resources. They may demonstrate their inquiry by:

• Making an object from odds and ends
• Drawing or painting
• Creating a mural that represents their inquiry
• Constructing large-area structures
• Developing elaborate and extended plans that spin off from the initial project
• Role-playing
• Recording project events and progress in a journal
• Having peer discussions about their inquiry and the next steps.

Once children demonstrate their knowledge via various artifacts and interactions, the teacher can build upon their wonderings and shifting interests. Encourage children to ask a lot of questions and seek their own answers. Have them check answers and notes against reference materials, pamphlets, interviews with experts, and readings. They can use the Internet and videos to gather information as well. Be sure to update the K-W-L process throughout phase two, and check progress against state standards (if required).

Phase three: Project in transition. I like the word "transition" to describe this phase because project work usually is a generative process. One project leads to another project, which leads to another. Phase three is an important phase, because in this phase the project begins to change, based on what children have learned. By now, their inquiry likely will result in new directions, shifts, and spin-offs from the original project. As projects transition they can:

• Splinter—children continue to investigate the original topic (school kitchen), but add related inquiries to it (school cafeteria).
• Shift—children may use the same basic project concept, such as "Shelters provide protection for animals," but shift the focus to another related concept, such as "Shelters also provide protection for people."
• Serve another purpose—children may use their project artifacts for completely different purposes, such as when a large cardboard house they created is recycled to serve as a children's bookstore in the corner.
• Fizzle out—children's interests in the project slowly fizzle. They show little or no interest in splintering or shifting their foci.
• End—children vote to terminate the entire project. They may start fresh with a new project, or they may need a break from project work.

Second-Grade Social Studies Project on "Shelters"
A 2nd-grade social studies project on "shelters" provides an excellent example of guided inquiry

using projects. The project can be part of an overall program and the usual school curriculum.

Rationale and background. Projects should be based on topics that relate to children's immediate world (e.g., fire truck, school bus), not on topics they cannot directly investigate (e.g., rain forest). An example of an immediate-world topic is "homes." I wanted to use homes as a project topic when I worked in the inner city, but many children didn't have traditional homes; some children, in fact, were homeless. Therefore, an open-ended topic that encompassed homes—shelters—seemed promising.

A shelter can be any physical structure that provides protection, for animals as well as people. Allowing children to tailor their investigations to either animal shelters or people shelters empowers them to make a choice with which they feel comfortable. At the beginning of the shelters project, one girl wanted to study only animal shelters as she did not have a consistent place in her life she called "home." After a few weeks, however, she helped peers with their people shelters.

Main project concepts. Because children's inquiry focuses on in-depth investigations, they should be learning main concepts, ideas, and messages that guide them throughout the project's life. The main concepts for the "shelters" project are:

- A shelter provides protection for animals and people.
- Shelters exist in many different structures, such as apartments, houses, and cars.
- Animals and people need different types of shelters depending on the environment, location, and needs of the people or animals.
- Shelters are made using different materials and with help from many people.
- Shelters have different features to them, such as size, shape, space, and sensory qualities (e.g., light fixtures, places to sleep, places to eat, and even transportation abilities).

Standards connections. After identifying the main concepts, I connected them to relevant state standards. Some teachers prefer to start with a standard. I believe that responsive teaching means starting with the children, and then matching their needs to the standards. With developmentally appropriate instruction, such as inquiry learning and projects, "fitting in" the standards is easy. Figure 2 includes a few examples of Arizona's and California's standards for literacy, mathematics, and social studies as they relate to the shelters project.

Objectives. With both concepts and standards in mind, I could develop objectives for the project. The first part of each objective is a previously identified main concept. The main objectives are:

- Students will learn that a shelter provides protection for animals and people, by participating in whole-group discussions and field trips that highlight protective aspects of shelters.
- Students will learn that shelters exist in many different structures, by investigating and creating different types of shelters.
- Students will learn that animals and people need different types of shelters depending on the environment, location, and needs of the people and animals, by brainstorming the different types of shelters and conducting follow-up field trips and interviews with experts in these areas.
- Students will learn that shelters are made using different materials and with help from many people, by planning and constructing various shelters.
- Students will learn that shelters have different features to them, such as size, shape, space, and sensory qualities, by adding physical details to their shelters.

Shelters project time frame. This project unfolded over a four-week time frame. The weekly planning chart in Figure 3 represents a typical project week. The week's structure did vary, however, depending on children's interests and unforeseeable events. The activities listed are general because each project day resulted in different tasks and outcomes.

CALIFORNIA AND ARIZONA 2ND-GRADE STANDARDS EXAMPLES
SHELTERS PROJECT

	Social Studies	*Literacy*	*Mathematics*
California	*Area: People Who Make a Difference* 2.2.1: Students demonstrate map skills by describing locations of people, places, and environments; locate on a grid system geographic features in their neighborhood [Project Concept 3] 2.4.3: Students understand basic economic concepts and their individual roles; understand how limits on resources affect production and consumption [of materials] [Project Concepts 3,4,6]	*Area: Reading* <u>Decoding</u> 1.0.1.5: Correctly use regular and irregular plurals [Project Concepts 1-6] <u>Comprehension</u> 2.0.2.4: Ask clarifying questions about essential textual elements of exposition (why, what if, how) [Project Concept 6] 2.0.2.7: Interpret information from diagrams, charts, and graphs [Project Concepts 2,5,6] *Area: Writing* <u>Research</u> 1.0.1.3: Understand the purposes of various reference materials [Project Concept 6] <u>Speaking</u> 2.0.2.2: Report on a topic with facts, details, drawings from several sources [Project Concepts 1,6]	*Area: Number Sense* 4.0.4.2: Recognize fractions of a whole and parts of a group (e.g., one-fourth of a [window pane]) [Project Concepts 4,5] *Area: Measurement/ Geometry* 2.0.2.2: Put shapes together and take them apart to form other shapes [Project Concepts 2,5]
Arizona	*Area: Civics/Government* 2SS-F1, PO2: Describe varied backgrounds of people living...in one's school and community [Project Concepts 1,3] *Area: Economics* 4SS-F2, PO3: Describe the characteristics of production and exchange, with emphasis on [people who] manufacture, transport, and market goods and services. [Project Concept 4]	*Area: Reading* 2.a Foundations: Use word recognition and decoding, and context clues to comprehend written selections [Project Concepts 1,6] *Area: Writing* 2.1.a-g Foundations: Use the writing process (e.g., mapping, brainstorming, K-W-L) to complete effectively a variety of writing tasks [Project Concept 6]	*Area: Number Sense* 1.1.a-f Foundations: Use numbers in physical models, drawings, word names, and symbols [Project Concepts 2,5] 5.1.a, b Demonstrate that a single object has different attributes (length, height) that can be measured in different ways [Project Concepts 2,5]

Figure 2

WEEKLY PLANNING CHART FOR 2ND-GRADE SHELTERS PROJECT

Monday	Tuesday	Wednesday	Thursday	Friday
Morning Journals Open Discussions	Morning Journals Open Discussions &/or Project Talk	Morning Journals on Projects Project Talk	Morning Journals on Projects Project Talk	Morning Journals on Projects Project Talk
District Curriculum (a.m.) *Lunch*				
Other activities	Other activities	**Project "PreBrief":** Whole group planning; KWL; reflections; question development; clarifying; evaluating; shifting foci, plans and interests; align to concepts and standards	**Project "PreBrief":** Whole group planning; KWL; reflections; question development; clarifying; evaluating; shifting foci, plans and interests; align to concepts and standards	**Project "PreBrief":** Whole group planning; KWL; reflections; question development; clarifying; evaluating; shifting foci, plans and interests; align to concepts and standards
Other activities	Other activities	**Project Implementation:** Investigation, research, construction, creation, field trips, guest visitors, revisiting photographs and documentation of project, role play, use of project artifacts, develop new ideas for project's direction	**Project Implementation:** Investigation, research, construction, creation, field trips, guest visitors, revisiting photographs and documentation of project, role play, use of project artifacts, develop new ideas for project's direction	**Project Implementation:** Investigation, research, construction, creation, field trips, guest visitors, revisiting photographs and documentation of project, role play, use of project artifacts, develop new ideas for project's direction
Other activities *Project time as needed*	Other activities *Project time as needed*	**Project "PostBrief":** Update KWL; reflections; question development; clarifying; evaluating; shifting foci, plans and interests; align to concepts and standards	**Project "PostBrief":** Update KWL; reflections; question development; clarifying; evaluating; shifting foci, plans and interests; align to concepts and standards	**Project "PostBrief":** Update KWL; reflections; question development; clarifying; evaluating; shifting foci, plans and interests; align to concepts and standards *Prepare for shift, termination, or/and celebration of project work*

Figure 3

Three phases of the shelters project. During each week of the project, the children had a set of child-generated questions to investigate and social studies concepts to research, while the teacher had social studies standards with which to monitor the work. The children began each morning by drawing and writing in a Morning Journal. This journal is a homemade journal made from blank paper and construction paper covers. Children would record project thoughts and draw the project's development and related activities in these journals. Multiple K-W-Ls were developed and updated throughout the entire project.

Phase One of the project lasted about one week, and focused on concepts 1-3 and related standards (see Figure 2). This phase centered on such questions as: What is a shelter? What kinds of shelters are there? Who needs shelter? What do shelters do? Where are shelters located? Children participated in simple research to answer questions and locate information related to project concepts 1-3. We also went on a field trip to the local zoo and searched for various animal shelters. While at the zoo, we took photographs of zoo shelters, which were enlarged and studied throughout the project. Related books, pamphlets, and pictures were among the data and information children used to begin their project.

Phase Two of the project lasted about two weeks, and concerned itself with Concepts 4 and 5 and related standards (see Figure 2). This phase focused on such questions as: What types of shelters can we make? What materials are used for different types of shelters? Are people shelters different from animal shelters? How? Why? What features of shelters are "necessary" and what are "luxuries"? Children continued to research and locate information related to project concepts 4 and 5. We took a walking field trip to view a nearby construction site, and hosted some guest speakers who build and/or sell shelters (e.g., home builders, sales persons from a pet store). Children continued their research. They read books and pamphlets, studied photographs and videos, interviewed experts, and updated their K-W-Ls. By this time, children were constructing various shelters using odds and ends,

boxes, wood scraps, and drawing materials. They made cat condos, doghouses, bird nests, birdcages, and three different types of people shelters. The birdcages hung outside an apartment house. The three people shelters were big enough for two or three children to use in their role play. They even made a library.

Phase Three of the project lasted about one week, and continued with concepts 4 and 5 and related standards. However, the momentum slowed down considerably when, during phase two, the children added the "library." The library took the children's focus in a different direction, and they shifted their thinking to "community" and away from the more narrow topic of shelters. I was pleased with this shift in focus because it allowed the children to add more social studies concepts and standards to the mix. Some children continued working on animal shelters and others worked on people shelters; now, however, some began developing a community. The community included: animal shelters, people shelters, a library, and a medical clinic. During phase three, the teacher and children had one large culminating celebration of their work (e.g., an open house to reveal their creations). We invited parents to visit the classroom on an informal basis throughout week five.

Closing Thoughts

Many administrators view social studies as one of those "irrelevant" content areas, to be left curbside while children hunker down and memorize alphabetic and numeric symbols. When social studies is covered in school, it usually is just that: covered. Teachers are pressured to present massive amounts of dates, names, and geographical and historical facts. Social studies is approached as a system for transmitting social norms (Spodek, 1974) and standardized facts. In this coverage-instead-of-mastery approach, children seldom *master* facts relevant to their daily lives.

Children need to learn by mastery, however. They need to glean information from daily events and tasks. According to Sternberg (1985), children need to learn more *practical knowledge*. To find out whether or not children are mastering practical knowledge, ask yourself these questions: Can children use what they learn? Does what they learn help them function in day-to-day life? Are children learning thoroughly what is before them, rather than becoming lost in a sea of symbols and facts? Do the children understand the relevance of what they are learning? I propose that teachers be concerned with social studies *relevance*, rather than social studies *coverage*. Social studies relevance is best accomplished through direct inquiry of the environment, whereby children *uncover* important information—such as with project work—rather than cover it.

References

Allison, J. (1999, September/October). Building literacy curriculum using the project approach. *Child Care Information Exchange,* Issue 129.

Hartman, J. A. (1993). *Review of the research on inquiry learning.* Cupertino, CA: Apple Computer Incorporated.

Helm, J. H., & Katz, L. G. (2001). *Young investigators: The project approach in the early years.* New York: Teachers College Press.

Spodek, B. (1974). Social studies for young children: Identifying intellectual goals. *Social Education, 38*(1), 40-52.

Sternberg, R. J. (1985). *Beyond IQ: A triarchic theory of human intelligence.* Cambridge, UK: Cambridge University Press.

Today's Classroom

Chapter 16
The Role of Autonomy in the Elementary Classroom

Lynn Kirkland,
University of Alabama at Birmingham

Jerry Aldridge,
University of Alabama at Birmingham

As misconceptions still abound about constructivism, this chapter will attempt to clarify some of the issues by addressing the following questions:

- What is a constructivist classroom?
- Who is a constructivist teacher?
- What do children do in constructivist classrooms?
- What is autonomy?
- Why are some children more autonomous than others?

What Is a Constructivist Classroom?

Constructivist classroom communities strive to promote children's cognitive, moral, and social development. These classrooms foster critical thinking and problem solving, rather than emphasize drill and recitation (Brancombe, Castle, Dorsey, Surbeck, & Taylor, 2000). Children are encouraged to make choices and decisions, and have time to experiment (DeVries & Zan, 1994).

Who Is a Constructivist Teacher?

The constructivist teacher works to develop reciprocal relationships with the children in the classroom, thus facilitating an atmosphere of understanding, fairness, and negotiation. For example, the children create and implement classroom rules that emphasize logical consequences rather than punishment. If a child makes a mess in the art center, then that child is responsible for cleaning up the mess.

What Do Children Do in a Constructivist Classroom?

Children in constructivist classrooms actively participate in the construction of knowledge. By fostering children's autonomy, teachers promote independence and self-governance. By minimizing adult authority, and giving children a voice in establishing the curriculum, environment, and rules of the classroom, teachers help children develop their ability to make decisions.

This process begins on the first day of school, when children participate in the creation of the classroom environment, provide ideas for curricular topics, and co-author rules for classroom management. Such participation in conceiving the classroom community helps children establish their place in the democratic process (Kohn, 1996). For example, children's ideas about topics they will study during the school year can be written on a chart tablet, which the teacher can consider when curricular decisions need to be made. Children might vote to decide on classroom "jobs," such as zookeeper, meteorologist, gardener, etc.

What Is Autonomy?

Piaget (1948/1973) described autonomy as the ultimate aim of education. In Piagetian theory, autonomy means the ability to think for oneself and to decide between right and wrong in the moral realm, and between truth and untruth in the intellectual realm, by taking relevant factors into account, independently of reward and punishment. (Kamii, 1992, p. 9)

Why Are Some Children More Autonomous Than Others?

Principles of teaching that directly relate to the development of autonomy can be examined through three different relationships—children and adults, children and peers, and children and learning (Kamii & DeVries, 1980).

In the first relationship, between children and adults, adult authority is minimized as much as possible. An atmosphere is developed that allows the adult and child to exchange points of view in a nonthreatening environment. When children have opportunities to negotiate, they build on this ability.

The use of choice is an indicator that the relationship between a teacher and child is becoming autonomous. Kohn (1993) asserted that children who are allowed to make decisions are more engaged in their learning. He encouraged the use of experiences that build decision-making skills and the inclination to use them. Setting up the classroom environment in a collaborative fashion with the children can offer them more choices about their schooling. Teachers also can give children choices in terms of the selection, production, and implementation of curriculum.

Relinquishing the use of rewards and punishment requires teachers to acknowledge, and reconsider, their use of power (Kohn, 1993). When controlling children through the use of rewards and punishment, there is no opportunity for children to make decisions based on their own thinking.

Relationships between children and their peers also can foster autonomy. When children exchange points of view with their classmates, they begin to coordinate points of view. As children take into account other children's ideas, they are more able to clarify their own. When children are unable to work out equitable solutions for conflicting ideas, the constructivist teacher can encourage

children, through effective questioning, to consider and clarify alternative solutions (Brooks & Brooks, 1993).

Finally, children's relationships to learning also can facilitate their development of autonomy. According to constructivist theory, children who are encouraged to think for themselves develop an intrinsic motivation for learning. Constructivist teachers do not believe that children "discover" all types of knowledge on their own. Although Piaget's theory does encourage children to be mentally active, he makes a clear distinction between discovery and invention. Rules of a game are an example of this distinction. Young children are unable to "discover" the rules of a game, but they can "invent" rules once a teacher has introduced them to the game and stated its specific rules.

Seefeldt and Barbour (1997) describe techniques that teachers can use to encourage autonomy in children:

- Have a clear understanding of who will be making decisions in the classroom
- Take into consideration individual children's needs
- Plan wisely for routines and smooth transitions in the classroom, to help avoid possible confrontations
- Allow children an opportunity to solve a problem that arises in the classroom, and intervene only when necessary
- Know the emotional and social needs of the children well enough to make informed decisions about if, and when, it is necessary to intervene
- Vary groupings during the school day, so that children develop increasingly complex social abilities to cooperate and participate within a group.

Some cultures and families view interdependence, rather than autonomy, as a more appropriate way to interact with children (Delpit, 1995; Hsue & Aldridge, 1995; Williams, 1994). However, the goals of autonomy and interdependence do not have to be mutually exclusive.

These roles can complement, rather than conflict with, each other. Interdependence and group membership can be promoted through classroom experiences such as work committees, small-group work, and class meetings. A balance of experiences fostering both autonomy and interdependence in children can promote continuity between the home and school.

The role of autonomy in the classroom is multifaceted. As we progress into the 21st century, we encourage teachers to critically examine the importance placed on autonomy in diverse classrooms, in order that they may work toward achieving equitable and effective learning environments.

References

Branscombe, N. A., Castle, K., Dorsey, A. G., Surbeck, E., & Taylor, J. B. (2000). *Early childhood education: A constructivist perspective.* Boston: Houghton Mifflin.

Brooks, J. G., & Brooks, M. G. (1993). *The case for constructivist classrooms.* Alexandria, VA: Association for Supervision and Curriculum Development.

Delpit, L. (1995). *Other people's children: Cultural conflict in the classroom.* New York: The New Press.

DeVries, R., & Zan, B. (1994). *Moral classrooms, moral children: Creating a constructivist atmosphere in early education.* New York: Teachers College Press.

Hsue, Y., & Aldridge, J. (1995). Developmentally appropriate practice and traditional Taiwanese culture. *Journal of Instructional Psychology, 22,* 320-323.

Kamii, C. (1992). Autonomy as the aim of constructivist education: How can it be fostered? In D. G. Murphy & S. G. Goffin (Eds.), *Project construct: A curriculum guide* (pp. 9-14). St. Louis, MO: Missouri Department of Elementary and Secondary Education.

Kamii, C., & DeVries, R. (1980). *Group games in early education: Implications of Piaget's theory.* Washington, DC: The National Association for the Education of Young Children.

Kohn, A. (1993). Choices for children: Why and how to let students decide. *Phi Delta Kappan, 75,* 8-16, 18-20.

Kohn, A. (1996). *Beyond discipline: From compliance to community.* Alexandria, VA: Association for Supervision and Curriculum Development.

Piaget, J. (1948). *To understand is to invent.* New York: Viking. (Original work published 1948)

Seefeldt, C., & Barbour, N. (1997). *Early childhood education: An introduction* (4th ed.). New York: Merrill.

Williams, L. R. (1994). Developmentally appropriate practice and cultural values: A case in point. In B. L. Mallory & R. S. New (Eds.), *Diversity and developmentally appropriate practices: Challenges for early childhood education* (pp. 155-165). New York: Teachers College Press.

Chapter 17
Safety in the Cybervillage:
Some Internet Guidelines for Teachers

Larry L. Burriss,
Middle Tennessee State University

Recent stories given great play in newspapers and in radio and television programs emphasize the dangers the Internet may pose to children. We have seen stories of suicides, kidnappings, and abuse that have occurred after children have accessed E-mail, chat rooms, and Web sites.

Just how frightened should teachers and parents be, and is there anything that can be done to prevent children from becoming victims of those who lurk in the dark corners of the Cybervillage? The problem here is actually twofold: there is both a lack of basic knowledge about the equipment (i.e., computers), and a lack of knowledge about the Internet.

Although computers have been in the classroom for several decades, many teachers remain uncomfortable using this technology. In addition, some schools do not provide the technical support teachers need in order to use these valuable resources.

Using a computer is not all that difficult. Yes, it requires learning some new words. Yes, it takes some time to read the instructions and then follow them. Yes, it is embarrassing when you have to ask a 9-year-old how to start the machine. Unfortunately, however, too many teachers confuse knowing *how* the machine works with knowing *why* it works. By way of analogy, most people have no idea why their family car works—what the oil really does or what actually happens when they press on the brake pedal. Yet they are quite comfortable driving a car. Using a computer is similar. If you can find the on/off switch, use a keyboard, and push a mouse around, you can use a computer. It is that simple.

Also, teachers may be uninformed about the Internet itself. The Internet seems to be a baffling array of addresses and sites, sounds and sights, information and cites. Again, it is simply a matter of spending some time getting acquainted with *how* to use the system, not necessarily learning *why* it works the way it does. Consequently, the first step towards cyber safety is to sit down, preferably with your students, and learn about the Internet.

Look at it this way: Suppose a child came to you and said, "I was down on Maple Street, going by that old blue house, and a stranger asked me to come inside to watch some television." And suppose you do not know where Maple Street is. Would you be too embarrassed to ask the child for directions? Of course not! Well, the Internet is the same way. If you do not know your way around, then ask. Facing a little embarrassment now could save a lot of grief later.

What can you do, then, to make sure the kids in your classroom are safe? For starters, teach children that the information superhighway is just like any other public street—you are going to meet some very nice people, but you also may run into some who are not so nice. Just as you would when walking along a public street, you have to be careful when you venture onto it.

Lesson one: Most children have been trained not to talk to strangers. The Internet may seem different, however, and so children may be lured into a false sense of security when the new "friend" on the Internet sounds just like the little friend next door. The Cyber-aware teacher will emphasize that students should not give names, addresses, or phone numbers to strangers, whether on the streets or on the Internet. Also, there is no need for children to tell Cyber-friends where they go to school or what they look like.

Other safety tips teachers can pass on to parents and students also involve plain common sense. What, for example, do parents do when little (or, perhaps, not-so-little) Susie or Johnny wants to visit a friend a couple of blocks away? The parent goes with the child for the first couple of visits. They talk with the parents. They see what the home life is like.

Just the same, when a child meets a new friend on the Internet, and the conversation goes beyond mere pleasantries, teachers should suggest that parents ask to "speak" with the parents on the "other end."

It may help to know that teachers do not need to do all of this alone. Recently, the Direct Marketing Association launched *Get CyberSavvy! The DMA's Guide to Online Basics, Behavior, and Privacy*. This guide offers a number of activities that can help both teachers and children learn their way around the Internet and set up rules to follow when visiting on-line sites. The activities are available at the DMA Web site (www.cybersavvy.org).

One of the benefits of the *CyberSavvy* program is that it allows teachers and students to set out explicit rules for on-line behavior. The following question-and-answer excerpt is typical:

"If I receive any E-mail messages that are scary, I will:
- Tell a parent, teacher, or other trusted adult immediately.
- Not respond to the message without my parent's or teacher's permission.
- Report the incident to my on-line or Internet service provider, or call the police if I feel threatened.
- Another choice: (type in your own choice)."

These rules can be made part of a contract between the student, the school, and the parents that also could include a user's code of ethics (Frazier, 1995).

Another source of good information for and about children is the American Library Association. The ALA has an extensive site that includes not only safety tips, but also information about "kid-friendly" locations that are educational, as well as just plain fun. The ALA on-line address is www.ala.org/parentspage. The mailing address is: ALA Public Information Office, Dept. P, 50 E. Huron St., Chicago, IL 60611.

One topic that always comes up in discussions of children using the Internet is obscenity and pornography. Just like in "real life" (as opposed to "virtual life"), it is important to get the facts. Yes, there are Web sites and news groups that are not fit for human consumption. I am not talking about art sites that show the unclothed people painted on the ceiling of the Sistine Chapel, sculpture sites that show Michelangelo's statue of David, or detailed medical sites. Rather, I am talking about the raw, sex-oriented sites that make headlines and conjure up images of perverts and child abusers lurking behind every keystroke. You name the activity, and there is probably a site that discusses it, shows it, and encourages it.

So what can you do to keep your students away from such sites? The only thing you can do is take some time to work with your children and make sure you know what they are doing, and how they are doing it.

Let us go back to the everyday world again. The local multiplex cinema is showing 12 films, ranging from *Bambi* to the latest "hack-'n-slash" thriller, and your class is going to visit the mall as part of a field trip. Do you allow 6-year-olds to roam unattended in the mall? What about a 10-year-old or a 15-year-old? If you would not allow a 6-year-old to visit the mall unescorted, do not turn her loose on the Internet. It is that simple.

What if you find a couple of 10-year-old boys in your class using the Yahoo search engine to look for the word "Maiden-form"? They are going to find some 300 sites dealing with warehouse management, the Advertising Education Foundation, "The Completely Unofficial Mystery Science Theater 3000" References Guide, dozens of outlet stores and malls, and, oh yes, lingerie. Are they going to see anything more risqué than the full-color newspaper ads for department stores they snicker over, or the life-like posters very publicly displayed in the windows of Victoria's Secret? Probably not.

At what point, then, does access to Internet sites become a problem? First, there are developmental differences between sneaking a quick peek at a lingerie home page, spending hours looking up Bali (which, by the way, yields several hundred sites related to the island, and one site featuring batik), and finding hard-core pornography. Each teacher will have to consider these access questions differently from an understanding of each child. If the child is spending hours and hours doing anything to the exclusion of everything else, however, there may be problems.

At any rate, the well-prepared teacher will find a way to appropriately discuss these subjects when they present themselves. The key here is the venerable rule, "Don't react, respond." Rather than reacting negatively, the teacher should use these "incidents" as learning opportunities for the students. These episodes could be used to discuss male/female differences, clothing, culture, health, and history.

The safety rules call for more direct monitoring of younger children than is necessary with older students. A class of elementary students on a trip to the museum may explore the halls freely, but the teacher will want the children to check in with them every hour or so. On the Internet, teachers in the classroom may need to check in with their children to see which sites they are visiting.

Fortunately, both Internet Explorer and Netscape Navigator provide "history" files that allow the teacher to "reaccess" sites that a user has visited. Again, teachers will have to learn how to use these files, and understand that if a child is accessing the Web yet there is nothing in the history files, then the student is deleting the site references. Then the question, and a rather serious one is "why is the child deleting the site locations?" As with all education, the goal is to provide meaningful guided experiences, while at the same time allowing an increasing degree of autonomy.

A practical solution to monitoring children's behavior on the Internet may be something as simple as making sure the monitors face into the room so the teacher can always see what is on the screen. Again, teachers need to look at the computer, and computer access, as being very much like television or public streets—you need to keep track of what is going on.

Summary

Despite some admittedly negative aspects of living in the Cybervillage, teachers can do some very positive things to make sure children are using this vast resource to its fullest potential. All they need to do is take some time to learn how the Internet works, and discover what is out there. Remember, there are vast differences in both learning and presentation between the traditional classroom experience and the Internet experience (Natale, 1995; Peterson & Facemyer, 1996).

Sure, the Internet offers a lot of games and silly locations to distract your students. It also offers an abundance of educational material that will provide relevant experiences for both teachers and students (Lindroth, 1996). For example, every major news organization has a site on the Web. These locations provide not only news, but also links to other interesting and educational sites. If, for example, you want to find more information about the sun for a science project, you could follow various links that start with coverage of the Hubble Telescope or the international space station. Links from news stories about tobacco will lead you to authoritative information in the fields of biology, medicine, and health.

The Internet has been compared to McLuhan's global village. As with every other village and town, some areas will present danger. With a little common sense and time, however, you can help protect your children and, at the same time, find lots of worthwhile places to visit.

References

Frazier, M. K. (1995). Caution: Students on board the Internet. *Educational Leadership*, October 1995, 26-27.

Lindroth, L. K. (1996). Internet connections. *Teaching K-8*, February 1996, 62-63.

Natale, J. A. (1995). Home, but not alone. *The American School Board Journal*, July 1995, 34-36.

Peterson, N. S., & Facemyer, K. C. (1996). The impact of the Internet on learners and schools. *NAASP Bulletin*, October 1996, 53-58.

Chapter 18
Benefits of Foreign Language in the Elementary School (FLES)

Kathleen Byrne,
Williamson County Schools, Tennessee

Foreign language instruction affects the ability of a country to communicate effectively in the international community. Through technological progress, our world appears to have become smaller, and it is common to have contact with many different cultures and languages. In the future, therefore, it may be considered a disadvantage to be monolingual. In this climate, foreign language learning becomes increasingly important.

Through foreign language learning students develop communication skills, learn about cultures other than their own, gain access to new information, develop insights into their own languages and cultures, and become participants in a multilingual community (Schrier, 1996). Families from all economic levels are beginning to realize the importance of foreign language learning as a way to interact meaningfully with different cultures (MacRae, 1957).

Foreign Language in the Elementary School (FLES)

Historically, U.S. public schools stressed the use and study of the English language. Children's native languages were not considered. Consequently, many language groups developed their own schools in efforts to maintain their native languages and cultures. In the 19th century, language groups began advocating for language support systems in the public schools that would meet students' bilingual needs.

There are numerous advantages to learning a foreign language. In fact, there are more bilingual than monolingual individuals in the world (Tucker, 1990). "Bilingualism has important cognitive benefits for individuals with respect to creativity, cognitive flexibility, and social tolerance; and it serves to expand occupational options" (Tucker, 1990, p. 14). "As [the United States] becomes increasingly dependent upon foreign trade, and, as international and political events exert more influence upon us, a largely monolingual population will be a handicap to our national growth and development" (Tucker, 1990, p. 14). Stern (1967) also emphasizes the need for foreign language study: "Language has been one of the great integrating factors producing group structure" (p. 7). Andersson (1969) believes monolingualism is a serious barrier to arriving at an understanding among ethnic groups within a nation. "Countries could greatly improve their social relations [among] linguistic groups and assimilate minority groups politically and economically if, from at an early age, all children acquired a useful control of a second language" (p. 46).

Today, foreign language study is supported and included within the regular curriculum in many U.S. public schools. In 1993, the National Commission on Excellence in Education recommended that foreign language and culture studies be placed with other curriculum subjects (e.g., mathematics, social studies, and technology) (Curtain & Pesola, 1994). With this addition of foreign language to the national core curriculum, Foreign Language in the Elementary School (FLES) is being redefined. The Goals 2000: Educate America Act calls for:

All students to achieve challenging high standards in a number of disciplines, including foreign languages. There is increasing evidence that these standards, part of a national agenda for foreign language proficiency and cross-cultural awareness, can be attained through an early start and extended sequence of foreign language learning. (Met, 1995, p. 76)

Through national support and research in foreign language acquisition, existing programs are expanding and new programs are developing.

From the moment of birth, children begin to vocalize. They have the ability to develop any spoken language; their external environment influences that language development. As children begin to produce the sounds of their native, or first, language, sounds that are not part of that language are not used and eventually are forgotten. In time, the child loses the ability to invent, practice, or imitate other sounds (Andersson, 1969). "The language environment influences the brain's selection of items appropriate to the specific language to which it is exposed" (Richard-Amato, 1996, p. 15). Research indicates that the structure of a child's first language is achieved by age 5 or earlier. The structure of the community is impor- tant when learning a second language. If students live in bilingual families or multilingual communi- ties, a second language may be a helpful means of communication (Stern, 1967).

In addition, the brain contains many highly complex structures that seem to come into opera- tion through an interactional process. These structures aid in language acquisition. As children mature and begin puberty, the brain appears to lose many of those complex structures (Omaggio Hadley, 1993; Richard-Amato, 1996). O'Malley and Chamot (1993) reported that children younger than 10 have more connections in their brains than do older individuals. At young ages, children learn almost unintentionally as the brain connects knowledge to be stored. This is one reason why adults seem to struggle with learning a new language.

There are both advantages and disadvantages to studying a second language before adolescence. Some advantages include promoting natural and well-defined pronunciation and providing a longer time for learning. In addition, the brain has a more effective influence on learning. Finally, students are able to expand their knowledge of language and culture. Disadvantages include students' inability to be consciously aware of acquiring the second language. Another disadvantage can be the confusion that results from mixing languages.

Older learners are more cognitively developed, possess a greater knowledge of the world around them, and have more control over input they receive (e.g., repetitions). Older learners also have first language strategies and linguistic knowledge that may be transferred to the second language. "The foundation of the second language is built on the first language" (Richard-Amato, 1996, p. 22). Prior knowledge of certain concepts and skills from the first language transfer to the second language. Some disadvantages for older learners include an increase in anxiety and inhibition, fear of making errors, and poor motivation and attitudes (Richard-Amato, 1996).

In contrast, young children enjoy learning a foreign language and tend to be curious about strange sounds. Young children are excellent mimics, especially at the early stages of language development. Children can duplicate correct pronunciation of a new language and are less self- conscious about producing strange sounds than are adolescents or adults. Suzanne Pahl (1992) re- ported that children from kindergarten to 2nd grade have a remarkable capacity for language learning. She points out that oral skills, in particu- lar, tend to be emphasized more at this level. When young children have mastered a second phonetic system, a lifelong benefit will be achieved. The learner will have a feeling of self-confidence and security. Therefore, students are motivated to continue their learning and achieve a higher level of proficiency in adulthood (Curtain & Pesola, 1994). Finally, children can benefit from a longer sequence of language study. This will enhance the learning of other languages (Lipton, 1989).

A Description of the FLES Program

Foreign Language in the Elementary School (FLES) programs, which have existed since the 1950s, encourage elementary and middle schools to begin an early introduction to foreign language. Basic characteristics of a FLES program include components that are sequential, cumulative, continuous, proficiency-oriented, and integrated into a K-12 sequence (Curtain & Pesola, 1994). A FLES program is usually taught at least every other day for approximately 75 minutes per week. Time is spent solely on learning the language. According to Curtain and Pesola (1994), the three major goals of a FLES program are "to acquire proficiency in listening and speaking (degree of proficiency varies with program), to acquire some proficiency in reading and writing (emphasis varies with the program), and to acquire an understanding of and appreciation for other cultures" (p. 30).

FLES supporters provide valid reasons for incorporation of the program into public schools. In the United States, many different cultures and languages coexist. Many U.S. cities have multilingual communities. In order to communicate daily with others, knowing a second language can be a necessity. International businesses operate because of bilingual and multilingual employees, and so knowledge of other languages and cultures is crucial in the international marketplace. The future holds many career choices and additional benefits for those proficient in a second language. Furthermore, "the introduction of a foreign language into a child's world helps him develop tolerance toward people different from him, and in the long run, contributes towards international understanding" (Vilke, 1979, p. 20). Exposure to many cultures allows children to experience differences without leaving the community.

Research suggests that the elementary school years may be the most appropriate time to begin studying a foreign language and global community issues. Children's attitudes toward different people appear to develop early, and may become more persistent with time. Attitudes toward other people also develop at an early age (Rosenbusch, 1992). "Children between the ages of 4 and 8 become increasingly aware of racial and ethnic differences, increasingly describe others in racial and ethnic terms, and show a tendency to accept and reject individuals on ethnic grounds" (Rosenbusch, 1992, p. 131). Fourteen-year-olds "were less receptive to learning about foreign people than were 10-year-olds, whose attitudes were more open and friendly toward people viewed as dissimilar to them" (p. 131).

The study of culture is critical to foreign language learning. By exposing learners to other cultures, educators hope to build children's respect, appreciation, and empathy toward people of different cultures and, in doing so, decrease monocultural outlooks. "To operate effectively in the social world children must learn to recognize, interpret, and respond to social situations" (Kostelnik, Stein, Whiren, & Soderman, 1993, p. 2). In the future, social interactions will no longer be limited to one culture. Therefore, it is important for children to be comfortable communicating with different cultures. Studying the culture of the language may spark new interest and add to the students' overall experience. As a student's goal when studying a foreign language should include the ability to understand and be understood in social and/or academic situations, language instruction should focus on real communication in situations where practice makes perfect (Richard-Amato, 1996). Social competence is acquired over time and is influenced by developmental, as well as experiential, factors (Kostelnik et al., 1993).

Within the FLES curriculum, the culture studies component provides children with knowledge regarding difference. FLES teachers provide children with the experiences needed to recognize other cultures, interpret expected actions, and respond effectively and appropriately across intercultural situations. With practice over time, children will attain a new level of social competency. Examples include greeting someone in another language or interacting with appropriate nonverbal communication (e.g., maintaining the appropriate amount of space between individuals when conversing).

Emotional supportiveness plays a critical role in the FLES classroom. Emotional supportiveness includes empathy, acceptance, authenticity, respect, and warmth (Kostelnik et al., 1993); these five components contribute to the relationship-building process. Empathy is the single most important element for allowing a person to respond to another's affective or emotional state by experiencing some of the same emotions. Acceptance is what every human being needs to gain confirmation from others. Authenticity can be found in those who are genuine with one another. FLES emphasizes the development of respect toward those having unique abilities, behaviors, and skills. Warmth, the manner in which people conduct themselves in social interactions, is also highlighted. Examples include showing an interest in others, as well as being friendly and responsive to them (Kostelnik et al., 1993). All five of these components are defined by Kostelnik et al. (1993) as essential for the helping professional. FLES promotes appropriate attitudes toward people of other cultures through such emotional supportiveness. "Attitudes toward self, the target language and the people who speak it, the teacher, and the classroom environment all have an influence on acquisition" (Richard-Amato, 1996, p. 78). If any one of the components is negative, learning will be undermined. This is why FLES learning environments strive to make students comfortable and to help them develop positive attitudes.

Self-esteem plays a major role in foreign language learning. Younger children are less anxious and less fearful of making errors. Thus, they are likely to feel more secure while trying to learn a foreign language than are older children or adults (Richard-Amato, 1996). Self-confidence reassures and motivates the learner to continue with language studies. Some children who struggle with basic subjects may excel in the study of foreign language. This success, in turn, helps motivate learners to master the other subjects (Omaggio Hadley, 1993).

Students who have high self-esteem feel good about themselves and evaluate their abilities more positively. Such students indicate high levels of learning. Low self-esteem may be associated with depression, anxiety, and maladjustment. Low self-esteem may generate poor learning (Kostelnik et al., 1993). Self-esteem is divided into three broad dimensions: worth, competence, and control.

"Children are sensitive to the attitudes people have toward them, and often adopt these opinions as their own" (Kostelnik et al., 1993, p. 77). Findings from a study on the effects of self-esteem and language performance in French indicate that those with high self-esteem generally performed better (Richard-Amato, 1996). High self-esteem, self-confidence, and self-security lead to an enhanced ability to acquire a foreign language. When a foreign language is studied at an early age, research indicates students' cognitive and divergent thinking skills are improved.

It is important to understand that learning a second language does not interfere in the acquisition of native language skills. Furthermore, learning a second language does not reduce the extent of average gain in achievement of basic skills being taught in the native language (Landry, 1974). In fact, children with two languages demonstrate greater flexibility. Children who are encouraged to switch from one language to another in their daily routine maintain adaptability and a willingness to change. Fluency, creativity, and problem-solving are associated with such adaptability and willingness to change. Sixth-grade FLES students who had studied a foreign language since the 1st grade scored higher on measures of divergent thinking than did non-FLES 6th-graders. FLES, with its emphasis on divergent skills, prepares students for lifelong learning (Landry, 1974). As Vilke (1979) states, "Intellectually, a child's experience with two language systems seem[s] to give the child mental flexibility, superiority in concept formation, and a more diversified set of mental abilities" (p. 20). Divergent thinking skills can facilitate success in the academic, social, and work environments.

Students show higher scores in other subject areas while studying FLES. Students who study a foreign language in 2nd through 6th grades achieve higher scores on standardized tests in English and mathematics (Lipton, 1989). Generally, students also perform better in reading and social studies when learning a foreign language. The native language also becomes better understood in terms of syntax, vocabulary, and structure (Curtain & Pesola, 1994). Students who averaged four or more years of foreign language study scored higher on the verbal section of the Scholastic Aptitude Test (SAT) than did students who had no foreign language learning. This research indicates that foreign language study improved both verbal and math scores on the SAT (College Entrance Examination Board, 1992).

FLES is an important and relevant part of elementary school. It is important to recognize that the teacher and the methods play key roles in determining students' progress in a FLES program. Furthermore, FLES in any school should be supported by the community and surrounding secondary schools. In keeping foreign language study continuous, all parts of language education should be involved and supportive of one another. This will help ease transitions between grades and promote students' progression.

The FLES teacher should be qualified and certified according to the state's board of education. Many programs were unsuccessful in the past because teachers were not qualified in the command of the language or in their knowledge of the elementary student (Shruman & Glisan, 1994). The program itself should contain a curriculum that connects the foreign language-speaking world with the students' own surroundings, both in and out of the classroom. The program also should emphasize communication, use various teaching methods, especially in the area of foreign language instruction, and relate to the established elementary education curriculum. Communication is perhaps the key to acquiring a second language. Over a period of time, FLES teachers need to focus on building their students' communication skills.

Conclusion

Studying a foreign language from an early age can help children develop high self-esteem, empathy, and acceptance for other cultures; develop the ability to interact appropriately with other cultures; improve scores in other subject areas; and increase divergent thinking skills. Learning a foreign language can open the door to a wide selection of career choices. Through continuous language study, children can become productive and empathic members of the global community.

References

Andersson, T. (1969). *Foreign languages in the elementary school.* Austin, TX: University of Texas Press.

College Entrance Examination Board. (1992). *College bound seniors. Profile of SAT and achievement test takers. National report.* New York: Author.

Curtain, H., & Pesola, C. A. B. (1994). *Languages and children, making the match.* White Plains, NY: Longman.

Kostelnik, M. J., Stein, L. C., Whiren, A. P., & Soderman, A. K. (1993). *Guiding children's social development* (2nd ed.). Albany, NY: Delmar.

Landry, R. (1974). A comparison of second language learners and monolinguals on divergent thinking tasks at the elementary school level. *Modern Language Journal, 58,* 10-15.

Lipton, G. C. (1989). *Practical handbook to elementary foreign language programs.* Lincolnwood, IL: National Textbook Company.

MacRae, M. W. (1957). *Teaching Spanish in the grades.* Boston: Houghton Mifflin.

Met, M. (1995). *Foreign language instruction in middle schools: A new view for the coming century. Foreign language learning, the journey of a lifetime.* Lincolnwood, IL: National Textbook Company.

Omaggio Hadley, A. (1993). *Teaching language in context.* Boston: Heinle & Heinle.

O'Malley, J. M., & Chamot, A. U. (1993). *Learner characteristics in second-language acquisition. Research in language learning: Principles, processes, and prospects.* Lincolnwood, IL: National Textbook Company.

Pahl, S. (1992). Youngest students to learn Spanish. *The Coalfield Process, 81,* 5-B.

Richard-Amato, P. A. (1996). *Making it happen.* White Plains, NY: Addison-Wesley.

Rosenbusch, M. H. (1992). Is knowledge of cultural diversity enough? Global education in the elementary school foreign language program. *Foreign Language Annals, 25,* 129-136.

Schrier, L. (1996). A prototype for articulating Spanish as a foreign language in elementary schools. *Hispania, 79,* 515-522.

Shruman, J. L., & Glisan, E. W. (1994). *Teacher's handbook: Contextualized language instruction.* Boston: Heinle & Heinle Publishers.

Stern, H. H. (1967). *Foreign languages in primary education.* London: Oxford University Press.

Tucker, G. R. (1990). *Second-language education: Issues and perspectives. Foreign language education.* Newbury Park, CA: Sage.

Vilke, M. (1979). *Why start early? Teaching foreign languages to the very young.* Oxford: Pergman Press.

Artistic Avenues

Chapter 19
Arts for All

Joanne M. Curran,
SUNY College at Oneonta

"Every child is an artist. The problem is how to remain an artist once he grows up."
—Picasso

There are two general approaches to incorporating the arts into elementary curriculum: arts-based education and integrated arts programs. Arts-based education programs have their foundations in the fine arts: music, visual arts, dance, and drama. For example, children learn music via instrument instruction, chorus, or music appreciation. The subject matter is music. In integrated arts programs, however, the fine arts are used as a means of supplementing instruction in the more traditional subjects of reading, writing, arithmetic, social studies, and science; regular classroom teachers look for ways to incorporate the fine arts into the curriculum. Both instructional approaches can be effective when the curriculum is carefully planned and implemented.

Arts-based education has a long history in the United States. As the numbers of children attending schools increased and budgets tightened, however, the first programs to be cut were the arts. Schools had to make difficult decisions about which programs to support, and many arts programs were not maintained. Advocates for arts programs have worked long and hard to have them reinstated in the schools. Such efforts have received support from both public programs, including the National Endowment for the Arts, and private sources, including the Getty Foundation.

More recently, attention has focused on how to integrate the arts into regular classrooms. Preliminary attempts placed great demands on classroom teachers because they were not prepared to teach arts courses, nor did they have experience in the arts themselves. Short-sighted plans to integrate the arts led to a further decline in arts-based education programs. Today, as a result of the support from public and private agencies, teachers and artists are working together to develop appropriate arts-based programs that are fully integrated into the curriculum. The purpose of this chapter is to describe ways to develop quality arts-based education programs that can be implemented across the elementary school curriculum.

First, teachers and other school professionals need to be able to discuss the benefits of an arts-based curriculum. Second, schools must have additional financial support to provide for arts program. Finally, families and communities that provide that support must recognize the value of the programs.

The purpose of arts-based education is to provide all children and youth with knowledge of, and skills in, the arts. A report from the National Endowment for the Arts (1988) cites the following benefits of arts-based education:

• Giving children and youth a sense of civilization and their place within their own culture (i.e., teaching cultural literacy)
• Fostering creativity
• Teaching effective communication
• Providing tools for critical assessment of what is produced by self and others.

Becoming Culturally Literate

By working together on arts projects, children learn how to overcome stereotypical thinking about groups different from theirs, how to build community, and how to recognize the value of traditions from different cultural groups (Wolf, 1983). Artwork provides a glimpse of what any particular social group values and, therefore, provides a means of identifying and expressing our own values as well as recognizing and understanding those values of other cultural groups. Children learn to respect others' work and to respect the process of creating those works when they are given the opportunity to explore the arts (Jalongo, Stamp, & Hall, 1997).

Working within the framework of the arts also allows full and equal participation in a classroom for students who are not yet proficient in English. A California program called SUAVE (Socios Unitas para Artes Via Educacion), an arts-integrated approach to teaching and learning, helped increase multilingual students' self-esteem, confidence, and motivation to learn (Goldberg, 1998). Social studies programs are often the first to completely integrate arts into the curriculum.

Fostering Creativity

While creativity is a basic requirement in most disciplines, it is most commonly associated with the arts. Music, drama, dance, and the visual arts all give special attention to the creative process within their specific disciplines. As creativity skills historically have served as core skills for the arts, teachers of the arts have the most experience in developing these skills in children and youth. Traditionally in education, teachers have had to split their attention between process and product; arts teachers focus more on process than product. Experts in the study of creativity agree that one cannot be creative without sufficient knowledge in a particular area, but some freedom or place for the imagination is equally critical.

Because everyone is creative, in just the same way that everyone is intelligent, arts-based education advocates promote the idea of teaching the arts to all, not simply to gifted and talented students. We may vary in terms of degree, but we all have potential! People who believe that they are not creative are generally employing a limited definition of the term. Creativity is the ability to take raw material and turn it into something new and relevant. Creativity is the ability to see possibilities where they are not obvious. Creativity is not simply being artistic; it is an attitude that acknowledges many routes to a goal and, when one route is blocked, finds an alternative route. Creativity is problem solving and taking calculated risks to achieve the goal. Creativity is seeing the world from a different point of view, and sharing that view with others in ways they can understand. Thus, teaching and learning are both significant creative acts.

We can foster creativity by providing classroom activities that offer children opportunities to learn to trust their own experiences. By deferring judgments (especially grading), teachers can assist children in learning to think more fluently, flexibly, and originally (Torrance, 1970). Thinking fluently means to generate many ideas for solving a problem. Thinking flexibly means to generate ideas in more varied categories (thus the current catchphrase, "thinking outside the box"). For example, when asked to think of all the kinds of transportation modes one could use to get from home to school, children's responses might only reflect automotive types of travel. A flexible response would be to include solar-powered modes, or animal-driven modes. To think originally is to create an idea that is unusual—that few others generate. Thinking originally requires taking a risk. New ideas often are ridiculed, but the rewards for taking a risk are great. Ask anyone who owns a patent on a useful invention! When responses are not immediately rated as correct or incorrect, children feel more comfortable thinking fluently, flexibly, and originally.

Within the arts disciplines, attention is given to developing freedom of expression prior to developing the skills of criticism. These skills can be fostered within any subject by adjusting the kinds of questions posed. For example, asking students to think of all possible reasons for a historical event, asking students to think of all possible ways of dividing a pizza, or asking students to think of all possible settings for a story will provide a sense of freedom with respect to traditional school subjects.

Teaching Effective Communication

Meaning in the arts is communicated through medium, form, and content. The medium may be music; a form of visual art such as sculpture or painting, dance, or drama; or the written word. Within each media, a particular form can be used—such as patterns of musical notes in a song, patterns of movements in a dance, or the structure of words to make a poem. The content is the subject matter of the piece. The combination of medium, form, and content enables children to create meaningful expressions of their own experiences and to interpret meanings expressed by others (Jalongo, Stamp, & Hall, 1997). The arts also focus on teaching children to pay attention to individual elements. For example, Suzuki methods of learning to play violin are based on attending to the sounds of the song and the sounds of the strings. The ability to observe, to listen, and to articulate in a variety of media enhances children's abilities to communicate. Young children can use arts media for expression and communication when their verbal skills are not yet adequate to the task (Wachowiak & Clements, 2000). Becoming sensitive to patterns in art forms easily translates to becoming sensitive to patterns in science and mathematics. Nonverbal expression often leads to more eloquent verbal expression, because the writer can describe images more intensely.

Becoming Arts Critics/Critical Thinkers

The creative arts require a combination of knowledge, imagination, and evaluation. Providing information so that children develop a knowledge base is critical. Some information can be transmitted, some information can be discovered, and some information can be shared. The important factor is that children are guided to operate from what they know. Once they have this base, they require the freedom to think about it imaginatively. We cannot lock them into a "right answer" mode of thinking. Yet, they also need some reins on their imagination. There is a difference between being

imaginative and being bizarre. Learning to develop criteria for evaluating whether or not a product is satisfactory is important. Teachers and artists can work together to develop these criteria. One principal attributed the gains made by students in an integrated arts program especially to the development of art criticism skills (Chapman, 1998). The children were able to look at art in an analytic way, and they were able to transfer that skill to other disciplines.

Teaching and learning critical thinking requires trust among students, artists, and teachers. Teachers trust that children have the capacity to think critically, develop new ways of learning, and make connections between their experiences and the materials they are learning in school. Teachers of the arts are trained to help children develop skills within their disciplines and to think critically about that discipline. Elementary teachers are trained to assist children in learning across disciplines and to bring a sense of holistic education to the partnerships.

In recent years, schools have been asked to provide a wide variety of services. In order to meet those demands, funds must be reallocated. Funding for the arts is one of the first budget items to be cut, especially for programs that serve the total student body. Yet, the National Endowment for the Arts (NEA) and other arts advocates continue to demonstrate the power of the arts in promoting learning in all domains. The NEA Web site (www.nea.gov) recommends ways to find funding for arts programs, and provides many specific ideas for integrating the arts.

Finding a Place in the Elementary Curriculum

Integrating the arts into elementary curriculum is not a new or controversial idea. Plenty of evidence demonstrates that educating children in the fine arts and integrating fine arts to teach all school subjects is a good idea (Eisner, 1998; Goldberg, 1998). Children need both direct instruction in the arts and opportunities to integrate the arts in the entire curriculum. Because teachers face many obstacles in putting an arts-based curriculum into practice, however, the arts too often are delegated to peripheral activities. The challenge is finding the best way to integrate the arts without sacrificing arts-based education programs, especially when teachers are faced with such a broad set of demands from students with a wide variety of skills and interests. Teachers and school administrators can work together to make fully integrated arts-based curriculums a reality by:

- Reminding the administration and the community of the value of arts in education
- Developing ways for teachers and artists to work and learn together
- Providing opportunities for children to learn about the disciplines of the arts, along with opportunities for incorporating what they learn into the standard subjects.

Remembering the Value of Arts Education in the Face of the Standardized Testing Movement

Teachers are under tremendous pressure to prepare children to perform well on standardized tests. Teaching to the test is becoming an acceptable behavior because the new tests require that students have developed certain skills as well as have acquired certain information. For example, document-based questions are now a part of many standardized social studies tests. In classrooms across the United States, teachers are preparing their students for the process of analyzing and interpreting documents—a skill that will be necessary to pass the standardized tests. The same skill is also a core skill in the arts, via arts criticism.

IDEAS FOR INTEGRATING THE ARTS

Blecher, S., & Jaffee, K. (1998). *Weaving in the arts: Widening the learning circle.* Portsmouth, NH: Heinemann.

Cornett, C. E. (1999). *The arts as meaning makers: Integrating literature and the arts throughout the curriculum.* Upper Saddle River, NJ: Merrill/Prentice Hall.

Erickson, K. L. (1995). *Integrated units in a dramatic framework.* Evanston, FL: Creative Directions.

Erion, P. (1997). *Drama in the classroom: Creative activities for teachers, parents & friends.* Fort Bragg, CA: Lost Coast Press.

Griss, S. (1998). *Minds in motion: A kinesthetic approach to teaching elementary curriculum.* Portsmouth, NH: Heinemann.

Isenberg, J. P., & Jalongo, M. R. (2001). *Creative expression and play in early childhood* (3rd ed.). Upper Saddle River, NJ: Merrill/Prentice Hall.

Laughlin, M. K. (1992). *Literature-based art and music: Children's books and activities to enrich the K-5 curriculum.* Phoenix, AZ: The Oryx Press.

Meinbach, A. M., Rothlein, L., & Fredericks, A. D. (1995). *The complete guide to thematic units: Creating the integrated curriculum.* Norwood, MA: Christopher Gordon Publishers.

Merrion, M., & Rubin, J. E. (1996). *Creative approaches to elementary curriculum.* Portsmouth, NH: Heinemann.

Ryder, W. (1995). *Celebrating diversity with art: Thematic projects for every month of the year.* Glenview, IL: Good Year Books/HarperCollins.

CONTACTS FOR HELP IN DEVELOPING INTEGRATED ARTS PROGRAMS

Getty Education Institute for the Arts
1200 Getty Center Drive
Suite 6000
Los Angeles, CA 90049-1683
www.artsednet.getty.edu

National Endowment for the Arts
Arts in Education Program
1100 Pennsylvania Avenue NW
Washington, DC 20506
www.nea.gov

Figure 1

While some states have included the arts in their curriculum objectives, the time allotted to arts education remains limited. In the pressured climate of preparing for standardized tests, teachers and school administrators sometimes are reluctant to take too much time away from direct instruction. Schools that have taken a chance and developed fully integrated arts education programs, however, report gains in standardized scores (Catteral, 1995; Chapman, 1998; College Entrance Examination Board, 1996; Goldberg, 1998).

Through arts-based projects, children develop imagination and aesthetic understanding; learn the basic skills of reading, writing, and mathematics; and gain a sense of classroom community (Wolf, 1983). We know that, developmentally, young children are not yet fluent in language and that their first cognitive acts are based more on perception than logic (Piaget, 1959; Wachowiak & Clements, 2000). Providing opportunities for young children to develop perceptual skills early will enhance the development of all subsequent skills. Children in arts-based programs have opportunities to learn how to learn in ways that enhance their chances for success; they develop understandings of themselves and their world using a variety of media.

Teachers and Artists Working Together

Teachers may be interested in including arts in their classroom curriculum, but feel justifiably unprepared to teach art, music, drama, or dance. As teachers' comfort and confidence with the arts vary widely, so do children's. Children as young as 7 or 8 may decide whether or not they can effectively communicate via the arts; too often, they decide that they cannot (Kindler, 1993). When attempting to integrate art into classroom curriculum, teachers may have to overcome their own sense of inadequacy with relation to the arts and then convince their students that the arts can be meaningful for them. This challenge is met most effectively when teachers and artists work together. Having an artist-in-residence is one way for schools to provide opportunities for such collaboration. The National Endowment for the Arts and private organizations that recognize the

value of the arts fund artists-in-residence education programs. In addition, classes can visit working artists, explore local museums under the direction of trained guides and docents, and communicate with artists via the Internet. Some artists work with curriculum planners, and new materials are being published for teachers to use in thematic, well-integrated units (see Figure 1). The Getty Education Institute for the Arts sponsors six regional institutes and has published a report, *The Quiet Evolution: Changing the Face of Arts Education*, to help schools develop arts programs.

Professional development programs in which teachers and artists work together to develop curriculum also have proven successful. SUAVE included inservice training and weekly in-class coaching by artist-educators. Teachers in this program not only were able to develop skills in integrating the arts into science, math, language arts, and social studies, but also learned how to teach some of the arts disciplines (Goldberg, 1998).

Opportunities for Children To Experience Arts Education

The primary challenge faced by teachers who want to integrate the arts is finding time in the curriculum. This can be done by working cooperatively with artists to carefully plan the method of integration. Acting out a Civil War battle may be an exciting activity, but the children also must be motivated to learn the relevant information. As teachers and artists continue to work together to develop such programs, the critical planning can be done by the artist and the critical implementation can be done by the teacher, or vice versa. Teachers and artists will need to allow children the time to develop artistic representations and, most important, they will need to learn how to talk about what the children are doing via the arts in ways that will help them generalize the skills gained and apply them to the rest of the curriculum.

Programs for arts integration require organization, cooperation, and willingness to take risks. The evidence is clear that well-planned integrated arts programs will lead to better learning, of both the arts and the basic curriculum. More important, perhaps, the learning will be an exciting process through which children discover themselves and their place in the world. The following poem was written as a group process activity in a 7th-grade drama class; it defines what an arts program creates for children.

A Space Where Anything Can Happen

A space where anything can happen:
a space to dream worlds
that we have yet to build;
a space to explore the limitless feelings
we all share . . .
the bond
that binds us all together.

A space
I can change
with the experiences of my life . . .
the imagined,
the feared,
the loved,
the hoped for,
the possible
and the impossible.

A space
where I can dare to be
the people I am
the people I see,
the people I fear to be
or the person I might become.

A space
where choices
are there for me to seize . . .
and dare!

A group poem (Wilder, 1977)

References

Catteral, J. S. (1995). *Different ways of knowing: 1991-1994 National Longitudinal Study Final Report.* Los Angeles: Galef Institute.

Chapman, R. (1998). Improving student performance through the arts. *Principal, 77*(4), 20-22, 24-26.

College Entrance Examination Board. (1996). *Profile of SAT and Achievement Test takers, 1990-1995.* Princeton, NJ: Author.

Eisner, E. W. (1998). Does experience in the arts boost academic achievement? *Art Education, 5*(1), 7-15.

Goldberg, M. (1998). Shifting the role of the arts in education. *Principal, 77*(4), 56-58.

Jalongo, M. R., Stamp, L. N., & Hall, H. (1997). *The arts in children's lives: Aesthetic education in early childhood.* Boston: Allyn & Bacon.

Kindler, A. M. (1993). Research in developmental psychology: Implications for early childhood art education practice. *Visual Arts Research, 19*(1), 16-19.

National Endowment of the Arts. (1988). *Toward civilization: A report on arts education.* ERIC Document No. ED 300287.

Piaget, J. (1959). *The language and thought of the child.* London: Routledge and Kegan Paul.

Torrance, E. P. (1970). *Encouraging creativity in the classroom.* Dubuque, IA: W.C. Brown.

Wachowiak, F., & Clements, R. D. (2000). *Emphasis art: A qualitative art program for elementary and middle schools* (7th ed.). New York: Longman.

Wilder, R. (1977). *A space where anything can happen.* Rowayton, CT: New Plays.

Wolf, D. P. (1983). The why of arts in education. In C. Hartnett (Ed.), *The arts go to school: An arts-in-education handbook.* Boston: New England Foundation for the Arts and American Council for the Arts.

Chapter 20
Musical Connections

Mary Palmer,
University of Central Florida

"With rings on her fingers
and bells on her toes,
She shall have music
wherever she goes."

These words from a traditional nursery rhyme may seem quaint in today's multimedia, high tech world in which it seems children would rather watch than do, and would rather dress like than sound like the stars. Yet music has an almost universal appeal and the potential to "grab" young learners. Therefore, it can be an effective instructional and motivational alternative; implementing a music-infused curriculum can enhance students' academic achievement. Indeed, there is much evidence to support the notion that music helps children learn and, equally important, helps children *want* to learn.

Psychologist Howard Gardner's theory of multiple intelligences has been a significant influence on education theory and practice. Musical intelligence is one of the eight discrete intelligences that Gardner identified (Gardner, 1983, 1999). According to Armstrong (1994), the greatest contribution of multiple intelligence theory is the suggestion that teachers must expand their repertoire of techniques, tools, and strategies beyond the typical linguistic and logical ones predominant in U.S. classrooms. When linguistic and logical/mathematical skills are the only measures of school success, the human potential of many students is left untapped. Hackett and Lindeman (2001) assert that music stimulates and enhances learning in every subject, and that students in schools with art-rich curricula excel in all subjects. For example, students in the New York City-based Learning To Read Through the Arts program have made substantial and long-lasting gains in achievement, and also display improved attitudes toward learning in general (Collett, 1991). Likewise, the Ashley River Creative Arts Elementary Magnet School (Charleston County, South Carolina), an ethnically diverse school, places the arts at the core of its curriculum, and students earn high scores on standardized achievement tests (Shuler, 1991). Music and the other arts contribute not only to demonstrated academic achievement, but also to academic satisfaction.

Incorporation of music into the elementary curriculum can be approached in a myriad of ways. This chapter will explore three of these: Brain Breaks, Esprit de Corps, and Curriculum Enhancement. In each case, the use of music may be incorporated discretely or used within an integrated framework.

Brain Breaks

Music provides a change of pace in the classroom. With music, children can move; play musical instruments (even homemade ones or objects from the environment that can create "found sounds"); sing; create their own lyrics, tunes, or accompaniments; or listen with a purpose.

Current research suggests that we can help the

brain function more efficiently through various activities, including:

- Changing what we are doing as frequently as every seven minutes (an occasional musical activity can "freshen" the children's brains)
- Standing (the children might stand to sing a song, do a movement, or perform a dance)
- Laughing ("silly" songs, musical jokes, or vocal sound play can make us all laugh)
- Having social interactions with others (music brings us together).

Thoughtful selection and use of music and music materials will help create a brain-friendly classroom environment. Music can be used to introduce a lesson, enliven the content of a lesson, or just provide a "break" from seatwork. When teachers treat the "brain break" as another opportunity for learning, children get a "2 for 1" value in learning.

Esprit de Corps

Music can help to bring people together and create a sense of belonging. Children get acquainted using various "name game" songs and chants. For instance, the "Cookie Jar" chant can be taught to the whole class and then be played by children in small groups. This song allows children to get acquainted with one another and gives them a sense of responsibility for participating in the chant. The experience can be varied by encouraging children to experiment with different vocal qualities (speaking, whispering, shouting, singing), expressive qualities (loud/soft; staccato/legato), and pitch changes (high/low) as they play, sing, and chant.

It is also helpful to develop a repertoire of songs to sing with the class. For example, teachers may wish to memorize 10 or 12 high-quality songs that are fun to sing and that advance the curriculum. Folk songs from around the world are good choices for this. These songs can be introduced during transition times, such as when students are lining up to go to lunch or the bus. They also can be integrated whenever a change of pace is needed in the classroom, such as when a break is needed from

doing math problems. These are great times to pull out your "hip pocket songs" and sing! These shared experiences will help to not only ease transitions, but also build a sense of community in the classroom.

Hearing a certain piece of music often invokes specific images, feelings, and events. Create some memories for your students by introducing them to great instrumental music. Select several pieces of classical instrumental music. Help the children identify the instruments, the style, and the expressive qualities. Selections such as *The Nutcracker Suite* by Tchaikovsky or *The Carnival of Animals* by Saint-Saens have varied sections and provide opportunity for a lot of learning. Don't be afraid to try jazz or ragtime or music of another culture. The goal is to extend children's exposure to a wide variety of great music. As children listen over time, they will hear more and more in the music. This deepening of listening skill will transfer to other experiences with music. In fact, practice with attentive listening will enhance children's attention to other learning as well.

Curriculum Enhancement

Choosing music and musical experiences to enhance children's music development while strengthening the total curriculum is an important goal. Music of high quality that will contribute to a lifetime of music appreciation is readily available and can be used for curricular enhancement. In language arts, for example, music can be used to accompany literature, set the tone for a story, or as a tool to support skill development (see Figure 1). Similarly, music can be used to support and enrich the social studies curriculum in numerous ways. Music can effectively convey the sense and feel of an era. Thus, the study of history is greatly enlivened through the incorporation of songs and dances popular during distinct time periods. Cultural appreciation is nurtured, deepened, and made more exciting through a study of people and their music (see Figure 2).

Conclusion

Music is a powerful catalyst for making lasting connections. Frequently neglected and too often

LANGUAGE ARTS CONNECTIONS

Shared reading
- Create charts or sentence strips of song lyrics. Ask children to read the lyrics. Once children are familiar with a song, mix up the sentence strips and ask the children to put them in the original order.

Discover rhyming words in a song; create new pairs of rhyming words
- Invite children to "fill in the blanks" with rhyming words as you sing "Oh, My Cat Is Fat." For instance, you sing "Oh, my cat is fat. She likes playing with a _____." (bat; rat) "Oh, my elephant is pink. He likes playing in the _____." (sink; ink)
- In "One Two Three Alary," children can use their own names to create new pairs of rhyming words. For instance, "One Two Three *Alary*, my first name is *Ben*; If you are a bit *contrary*, close your eyes and count to *ten*."

Practice verb conjugations in a question/answer song
- In the song "Going on a Picnic," children respond to questions such as "Did you *bring* the (hot dogs)?" with answers "Yes, I *brought* the (hot dogs)." When you change the song lyrics to "Going on a shopping trip with my Mom today . . .," children can practice different verbs ("Did you *go* to Walgreen's?" "Yes, I *went* to Walgreen's."). With the change in lyrics, children also gain practice in categorizing objects, events, etc. (Where would you go on a shopping trip? What would you see on a field trip to the symphony?)

Identify and dramatize the mood of a song
- The song "Five Little Frogs" has an upbeat, happy mood as the five frogs enjoy a day at the frog pond. Children will enjoy playing with facial expressions to show the frog's moods. As children dramatize the frogs jumping off the log into the pond, they will gain practice with number concepts (one-to-one ratio; subtraction.)

Create sound effects to enhance a story
- For the familiar nursery story of *The Three Bears,* you might assign a large drum sound for the Papa Bear, a tambourine for the Mama Bear, and a triangle for the Baby Bear. Each time a particular character appears in the story, that sound effect is played. Other sound effects may be added according to the content of the story. For instance, a vibraslap may represent the breaking chair; a guiro may represent the sleeping "guest."
- In *The Napping House* by Audrey and Don Wood (1984), the sleeping characters are introduced one by one. A surprise visitor (the wakeful flea) then comes to awaken the nappers. Assign instruments to represent each character. Children begin to play their instruments when their assigned characters are introduced in the story; once a character is introduced, children will continue to play their instrument. How they play their instrument (for example, soft/loud; slow/fast) will vary according to whether the character is sleeping or awake. (Some instrument possibilities: snoring granny = guiro or notched rhythm sticks; child = bell tree; dog = maracas; etc.)
- Invite children to create sound effects on instruments or with "found sounds" (using objects in the environment) to enhance the reading of stories that you are reading in class.

Use instrumental sounds to create a "soundscape" to enhance the mood of a story
- A "soundscape" is a rather continuous background accompaniment that enhances a story. Experiment with instrumental sounds to create the effect of a rainstorm. Read *Listen to the Rain* by Bill Martin and John Archumbalt (1988) and experiment with the sounds of different types of rainstorms. Shaking a piece of sheet metal (make sure that it has smooth edges!) and beating a drum will enhance the effect of the "hurly, burly" rainstorm, while light taps on a bell chime will suggest the "singing rain."

Enhance the oral reading of a story with background music
- First, identify the mood, culture, or time period of a story. Then, select instrumental music to match. Music that changes as the events of the story proceed will provide further enhancement of the reading experience.
- You might like to start with a folktale from a particular era or culture and play music of that time or place to accompany your reading. For instance, to accompany Cynthia Rylant's *When I Was Young in the Mountains* (1992), you may select a piece of Southern folk music played on the dulcimer and a fiddle.
- Elton John's "Funeral for a Friend" adds depth to the reading of *The Spooky Old Tree* by Jan and Stan Berenstain (1978).

Figure 1

relegated to the music teacher alone, music has the potential to enhance any classroom. Through the incorporation of song and dance, elementary teachers have the opportunity to enhance curricula, nurture a warm and joyful sense of community, and support the development of children's musical intelligence and other thinking skills. With all this, students of the 21st century may benefit immeasurably from the classroom teacher who does indeed "have music wherever she goes."

References

Armstrong, T. (1994). *Multiple intelligences in the classroom.* Alexandria, VA: Association for Supervision and Curriculum Development.

Collett, M. J. (1991). Read between the lines: Music as a basis for learning. *Music Educators Journal, 78*(3), 42-25.

Gardner, H. (1983). *Frames of mind: The theory of multiple intelligences.* New York: Basic Books.

Gardner, H. (1999). *Intelligence reframed: Multiple intelligences for the 21st century.* New York: Basic Books.

Hackett, P., & Lindeman, C. A. (2001). *The musical classroom: Backgrounds, models, and skills for elementary teaching.* Upper Saddle River, NJ: Prentice Hall.

Shuler, S. C. (1991). Music, at-risk students, and the missing piece. *Music Educators Journal, 78*(3), 21-29.

Music Materials cited are from *The Music Connection,* 2001, published by Silver, Burdett, Ginn. All songs are recorded on the CDs that accompany the textbook.
"One Two Three Alary" – Grade 2, page 30
"Going on a Picnic" – Kindergarten, page 80
"Five Little Frogs" – Grade 1, page 174
"Sweet Betsy from Pike" – Grade 4, page 166
"Che Che Koolay" – Grade 2, page 167
Beethoven: Minuet in G – Grade 2, page 60 (photos of children in period costumes).
"My Cat Is Fat" was composed by the author.

Children's Books Cited

Berenstain, J., & Berenstain, S. (1978). *The spooky old tree.* New York: Random House.

Martin, B. (1988). *Listen to the rain.* New York: Henry Holt.

Rylant, C. (1992). *When I was young in the mountains.* New York: Dutton.

Wood, A. (1984). *The napping house.* Orlando, FL: Harcourt Brace Jovanovich.

SOCIAL STUDIES CONNECTIONS

Enliven history through song and dance
- The spirit of our forebears is captured in the song "Sweet Betsy From Pike." Guide children to recognize the humor and the "stick to it" spirit of the '49ers through this re-telling of Sweet Betsy's travels from Pike County, Missouri, to California. In un-packing the song content, children will be able to create a map of Betsy and Ike's trip. They can determine how long the trip must have taken in the mid-19th century, as compared to today (using cars, planes, trains).
- You might re-create a "barn" party typical of those that the pioneers enjoyed. Invite children to join in the "play parties" (e.g., "Skip to My Lou") and square dances of early America.

Connect with cultural groups
- "Che Che Koolay," a call and response (follow the leader) song from Ghana, provides an introduction to an important musical form in Africa. Many children's recordings (see reference list) include authentic African instruments, such as drums, thumb piano, and shakers, to accompany the singing. Children will enjoy hearing and playing these instruments from Africa.

Create the "feel" of an era
- Show children a picture of people attending a formal "ball" during the 18th century. Invite them to imagine what it would feel like to wear those clothes. Encourage them to "try out" the clothes as they listen to 18th century dance music. Play "Minuet in G" by Beethoven. Guide children, wearing their imaginary 18th century ball clothes, to step elegantly with the beat of the music as they listen.

Figure 2

Chapter 21
Move It or Lose It:
Exploring the Benefits of Movement Experiences in the Elementary School

Nancy Hughes,
University of Central Florida

Do you remember when you first knew you wanted to be a teacher? I do. I would come home from elementary school, line up my stuffed animals, and teach away. My "students" would sit motionless, rapt with attention, hanging on my every word. This was the life, I thought. I couldn't wait to become a real teacher with living students. A number of years and a bachelor's degree later, I finally was allowed to teach a room full of living, breathing children. My, how different these students were compared to my stuffed animals. These children moved. And not a little; they moved so much I found it difficult to meet my primary objective, which was to teach. When I would call my students to gather on the floor for a large-group activity, the circle area became a professional wrestling mat. During *seat work* time, the students were everywhere in the room except their seats. Students were walking around, visiting the pencil sharpener, and . . . wiggling. Even a simple procedure like lining up at the door to go to lunch became a full body contact sport.

As an enthusiastic beginning teacher, I was confident I could find a solution. I observed classrooms taught by veteran teachers to discover the secret. What I saw in some other classrooms disturbed me more than all the movement in my classroom. Sure, children in some classrooms were sitting still—they were afraid to move. It seemed as if the teachers in these classrooms saw their role

as that of a drill sergeant. The desks were placed in rows and the children were not allowed to leave their desks. Furthermore, they were forbidden from turning around in the desks—even to pass papers to the students behind them. When these classes walked in the hallway they brought to mind soldiers marching in cadence. The teachers explained that the children had opportunity for movement during physical education class. While this may be true, recent surveys reveal that roughly only one-third of school-age children receive the minimum recommendation of 30 minutes of physical education, five days a week (Brink, 1995). Surely, I could find an alternative that lay between mass chaos and regimented order.

When I conducted a little research, I discovered why my current students were so different from my former stuffed animals. These living students had needs—and one of the most important was movement. Research findings show that active children think better and score higher on exams than their less active peers (Hannaford, 1995; Pica, 2000). After discovering the benefits of movement for children, I realized my choice was either provide an appropriate outlet for this need or be locked in a constant struggle with my class. I chose to provide the physical outlet. As my career has progressed from classroom teacher to university instructor, I have been able to support other teachers and student teachers in incorporating movement activities into the curriculum.

Brain Development Benefits

Physical activity not only modulates a student's brain for optimal alertness, it also prepares the brain physiologically for learning. Movement increases the oxygen and blood supply to the brain, which increases energy and allows students to maintain their alertness (Brink, 1995; Hannaford, 1995; Jensen, 1998). Along with the increase in oxygen and blood, the brain of a moving body is flooded with calming chemicals, called endorphins, that produce positive feelings of well-being and motivation (Jensen, 1998). An absence of these endorphins may result in negative behaviors like aggression, irritability, impulsiveness, violence, and recklessness (Sylwester, 1998). Finally, coordinated physical activity releases neurotrophins that increase the number of neural connections in the brain, which in turn results in higher processing of information (Brink, 1995; Hannaford, 1995). If I wanted my students awake, focused, and ready to learn, I needed to provide opportunities to move. As a byproduct of this movement, unwanted behaviors were reduced and the students were in a positive frame of mind. While recent discoveries regarding movement and brain development have focused on early development, studies using magnetic resonance imaging reveal that the brain's sensitivity to experience continues through age 18. This meant that movement activities would provide my elementary school students similar payoffs as those gained by younger children (Kolb, 2000). Pam Schiller (1999), in her book *Start Smart*, sums up the benefit of movement on brain development:

There are many studies that document the overall benefits of exercise, but the benefits for the brain are clear and simple: exercise increases the flow of blood and oxygen to the brain. People who exercise regularly have improved short-term memory and exhibit faster reaction time. Exercisers also demonstrate higher levels of creativity than non-exercisers. (p. 41)

Learning Styles and Intelligences

Teachers long have recognized that children have distinct learning styles—visual, auditory, tactile, and kinesthetic—developed through a combination of biology and experience (Green, 1999). As a result of teaching styles that limit children's movement, kinesthetic learners frequently are labeled as hyperactive and underachievers (Green, 1999; Pica, 2000). Providing learning environments that match these students' needs results in higher achievement and motivation. This became clear to one of my university students during a recent internship experience. One particular child seemed to have difficulty paying attention to lessons. When any music or movement activity occurred during the school day, however, the child was focused and engaged. One day, while the intern was conducting a one-on-one activity with the child, the classroom teacher suggested, "Maybe you should sing it to him." While the teacher's intent was to be facetious, the university intern recognized the unintentional relevance of the comment. If a child's preferred learning style is kinesthetic, we do a disservice when we require him or her to stay seated and still.

Beyond learning styles, Howard Gardner (1983) has identified at least eight different intelligences, one of which is bodily kinesthetic. While all individuals have the potential to learn, each person's predominant intelligence allows him/her to bridge into weaker academic areas through the use of this predominant intelligence. Students whose predominant intelligence is bodily kinesthetic solve problems through moving their body.

In my Observation and Assessment course, I ask the university students to identify a child in their internship placement who demonstrates learning or behavioral difficulties, and then to track this child using a variety of assessment tools. Many of the children who are chosen demonstrate an inability to focus on classroom lessons and a failure to complete assignments. As my students observe and track the child's daily behavior, they find that these children often are reprimanded for moving about, walking to the pencil sharpener, standing while completing seat work, and fidgeting. During this same course, the university students must teach a lesson based on Howard Gardner's theory of multiple intelligences. This lesson is designed to meet the needs of diverse learners based on their preferred intelligence and learning styles. Many of my students are surprised that the very same target children who have difficulty sitting still and focusing during a "traditional" lecture/seatwork lesson are the most engaged and participatory students during the multiple intelligences lesson.

As I recognized the advantages of including movement activities into the daily classroom routine, I wondered how to include them among the mandated curriculum requirements. Certainly, the easiest method would be to change the environment of the classroom. Reducing the restriction on free movement throughout the classroom and increasing the use of interest and learning centers would provide students with opportunities for movement. I realized that in addition to such environmental adaptations, a planned movement experience that integrated with and extended the subjects I already taught would be beneficial. In addition, considering the potential benefits to the students, I now believed that a break to move around could be the most important time of the day.

Integrating Movement Into the Curriculum
Integrating movement activities into the planned curriculum is a method that covers content and meets students' need to move. Many teachers who integrate learning activities around a central theme include kinesthetic activities, along with language arts, math, science, and social studies. A school district in Vancouver, Washington, incorporates movement elements (see Figure 1) into lessons that meet the national science standards. These teachers encourage the students to integrate movement as a method of understanding weather patterns, simple machines, volcanoes, and planetary relationships. For example, in a lesson on volcanoes, students might be asked to demonstrate with their bodies the shape of a volcano before, during, and after an eruption. Another activity would allow a child to demonstrate the timing and energy of the eruption (explosive, bursting, and fast), compared to the timing and energy of the lava flow (slow and flowing). After individual movement exploration, the students team up to role play movements for each volcanic element, such as the mountain, lava, ash, steam, trees, or animals (Thompson, 1998).

Problem Solving and Creativity
Ultimately, a long-range goal for our students is the ability to be creative problem solvers. This skill

---

MOVEMENT ELEMENTS

Space. The area available for movement. Includes personal space or general space (the classroom). Space includes the direction of movement (forward, backward, sideways), the level of movement (high, middle, low), the size of the movement (large, small, wide, narrow), and the pathways used (straight, curved, zigzag, crooked).

Time. The speed or change of speed of the movement. Includes fast, slow, accelerating, and decelerating.

Shape. The form or configuration the body takes during the movement exercise. Includes general shape (such as rounded or angular) and specific shapes (such as forming numerals or letters).

Flow. Describes the progress of the movement. Includes continuous and free-flowing movement (such as a kite) or bound, broken, and punctuated movement (such as a robot).

Force. Describes the energy of the movement. Ranges from strong, heavy, and forceful (such as a dinosaur's movement) to weak, light, and soft (such as a butterfly's flitting).

Figure 1

is critical for study of many academic subjects, and is a necessary life skill. Planned movement activities can increase the use of problem solving and creativity in an enjoyable manner. After an initial reading of a story or piece of literature, students could extend the experience by assigning roles and planning creative dramatics for the characters' movements. When used throughout the day, structured dramatic activities can stimulate students' thinking. Using the elements of movement, ask the students to move in a way that expresses:

Feelings . . . angry, disappointed, surprised, happy, or silly

Force . . . a floating feather, a falling asteroid, a floppy rag doll, a stiff toy soldier, an angry person, a cat stalking its prey

Time . . . a supersonic jet, a glider, a melting ice cube, an arrow being shot, bread coming out of a toaster, a yo-yo

Size . . . a bulldozer, a bicycle, a whale, a minnow.

Another activity is an adaptation of the traditional statue game. Students move throughout the classroom; when you ring a bell they form a specific shape using their bodies, such as a table, chair, globe, pencil, sharpened pencil, or pancake.

Transition Ideas

While my planned activities for the day would flow smoothly in my lesson plan book, I found that the students needed help shifting gears as they moved from one activity to the next. In addition, different times of the day presented additional challenges, such as lining up at the door to leave the room, walking in the hallways, and any time spent waiting. Using movement activities made these transition times easier to navigate. For instance, when asking my students to line up at the door, I gave a specific direction for movement in the line. For example, direct the children to:

Line up as if they are . . .
. . . carrying a football in a game and you are on instant replay slow motion
. . . walking barefoot on hot sand
. . . dribbling a soccer ball among players from the opposing team
. . . finishing an exhausting marathon.

For walking in the hallways, where some modicum of control is expected, I directed the students to move using a variety of locomotor movements (see Figure 2), such as sliding, jumping, hopping, creeping, and tiptoeing. On other days, I would design a verbal obstacle course for the students to follow. They had to listen closely to hear the change in locomotor movements as we made our way through the hallways. The hallway activity the students enjoyed the most was marching in cadence as they quietly repeated our class rap to keep everyone in step.

Even with careful planning and organized activities to encourage order while lining up and walking in the hall, time spent simply waiting is inevitable. It is helpful to keep a collection of movement activities on hand to fill this wait time. Since your class will be required to remain quiet and orderly during this wait time, non-locomotor activities (see Figure 3) fit this situation. Give your class directions, such as:

Shake like . . . Jell-O, bacon frying, you are very cold.
Twist like . . . a screwdriver, a washing machine, a wet dishrag being wrung dry.
Walk in place as if you are walking . . . on ice cubes, on a marshmallow, in gooey mud.

LOCOMOTOR MOVEMENTS

Crawl	Creep
Leap	Gallop
Walk	Hop
Jump	Slide
Run	Skip
Jog	March
Fly	Roll
Twirl	Tiptoe

Figure 2

Community Building

To create a positive learning environment that is conducive to cooperation and teamwork, teachers must provide opportunities to build camaraderie. Movement can develop creative problem-solving, communication, and cooperation skills (Thompson, 1998). Physical activities allow the students to work together in a meaningful way. Here are some directed community-building activities that students enjoy:

Unravel the Human Knot. A group of students (the more students, the longer it takes to unravel) stand in a circle. Each student grasps hands with two other students across the circle. The group then tries to untangle the knot without letting go of the hands.

Stay on the Line. The students stand on a masking tape line. The person at one end of the line must move to the other end without taking both feet off the masking tape at the same time. The other students help the student move down the line.

Back-to-Back Standup Game. Two students sit on the floor with backs touching and elbows interlocked. As a team, the pair attempts to stand up and sit back down without moving apart (Kranowitz, 1995).

Trust Walk. Students working in pairs attempt to navigate the classroom while one leads the other who has closed eyes.

Outside Play

Adults and children alike need a change of scenery after working for a long time at their desks. Adults may have the freedom to leave their office for a break outside to get some fresh air and take a walk. Children need time to engage in physical movement outside, especially since physical education time at many schools has been reduced or eliminated. Planned movement activities such as the following expand the benefits of outdoor time.

Red Light/Green Light. This traditional game allows for a great deal of movement, but also requires attention, careful listening, and self-control. Make the game more interesting by changing the locomotor movements (skipping, crawling, hopping), or make it a cooperative game by making the goal to have everyone to cross the finish line.

Who Let the Dogs Out? Using the song "Who Let the Dogs Out?" by the Baha Men, one person acts as the "dog catcher" while the remaining students (the "dogs") tuck a flag football flag into their waistbands, resembling a dog tail. As the music plays, the dog catcher chases the dogs and attempts to grab a tail (flag). If a dog's tail is stolen, he/she becomes the dog catcher. The dog catcher can choose a new locomotor movement as the game progresses (Pierog, 2000).

Crack the Whip. The class holds hands, forming a long line. The person on one end begins to run, leading the rest of the line. The leader changes directions, causing the line to double back toward the end. The students try to continue holding hands despite the erratic swings.

Inside Movement Activities

If time or weather prevents you from taking your class outside, a number of activities and games can be adapted for small, indoor places. These excellent activities will help to reenergize your students quickly after a long, tedious period of work.

Four Corners. Number the corners of your classroom. One person (It) hides his/her eyes while each of the other students chooses one of the corners. "It" calls a number and the students

---

NON-LOCOMOTOR MOVEMENTS

Stretch	Bend	Shake
Turn	Rock	Swing
Sway	Twist	Dodge
Wiggle	Fall	Pull
Push	Lift	Strike
Throw	Kick	Float
Wring	Bounce	Catch
Press	Slash	Wave

Figure 3

135

standing in that corner must sit down. The remaining students continue to change corners until one person is left standing. This person becomes the new "It" and the game continues.

Newspaper Toss. The class divides into two teams, separated by a strip of masking tape. Each group has one minute to make as many newspaper balls as possible. When the bell rings, each team tries to get all their newspaper balls onto the other team's side. When the bell rings again, everybody stops and counts newspapers. At the end of the game, each team tries to clean up their side first.

Space Ball. Cut off the leg of a pair of pantyhose and stuff the remaining part of the hose down into the foot. Tie a knot around the ball you have made in the toe. Have students toss the "space ball" to a friend or try to toss it into a basket in the middle of the room (Feldman, 2000).

Ball and Can Catch. Using an empty potato chip canister and a tennis ball, students bounce the ball and catch it in the can. Students can pair up to play catch, using two cans (Feldman, 2000).

Paddle Ball. Staple two paper plates together, leaving a space open for a hand to fit into the middle of the plates. Create a ball by wrapping scrap paper and masking tape together. Students can bat the ball individually or volley the ball in pairs (Feldman, 2000).

Mini-trampoline. Keep a small trampoline in your room for students who need to energize or release a little extra energy. Bouncing can also be helpful in reducing stress.

After implementing these movement activities with my class, I immediately began to see positive outcomes. Knowing that a variety of movement activities would be provided throughout the day, my students did not feel the need to move constantly during lessons or seat work. In addition, I was able to redirect the rough play that occurred during large-group times and that had previously dissolved into wrestling matches.

Too many students are asked to remain motionless throughout the school day and are punished for expressing their inherent need to move. Instead of telling students to be still, why not encourage them to move and learn? Remember,

mobility is central to much that's human—whether the movement of information is physical or mental. We can move and talk. Trees can't. Misguided teachers who constantly tell their students to sit down and be quiet imply a preference for working with a grove of trees, not a classroom of students. (Sylwester, 1998)

References and Resources

Brink, S. (1995). Smart moves. *U.S. News & World Report, 118*, 76-78.

Feldman, J. (2000). *Transition tips and tricks for teachers.* Beltsville, MD: Gryphon House.

Fishback, S. J. (1998). Learning and the brain. *Adult Learning, 10*, 18-22.

Gardner, H. (1983). *Frames of mind: The theory of multiple intelligences.* New York: Basic Books.

Green, F. E. (1999). Brain and learning research: Implications for meeting the needs of diverse learners. *Education, 119*, 682-687.

Hannaford, C. (1995). *Smart moves: Why learning is not all in your head.* Arlington, VA: Great Ocean Publishers.

Jensen, E. (1998). How Julie's brain learns. *Educational Leadership, 56*, 41-45.

Kim, K. (1995). Moving to learn. *Instructor, 104*, 66-69.

Kolb, B. (2000). Experience and the developing brain. *Education Canada, 39*, 24-26.

Kranowitz, C. S. (1995). *101 activities for kids in tight spaces: At the doctor's office, on car, train, and plane trips, home sick in bed.* New York: Skylight Press.

Kranowitz, C. S. (2000). Music and movement bring together children of differing abilities. *Child Care Information Exchange*, 57-60.

Landy, J., & Burridge, K. (1997). *50 simple things you can do to raise a child who is physically fit.* New York: Simon & Schuster Macmillan Company.

Pica, R. (2000). *Experiences in movement with music, activities and theory* (2nd ed.). Albany, NY: Delmar Thomson Learning.

Pierog, L. (2000, December 14). *PE Central.* www.pecentral.org/lessonideas [retrieved January 2, 2001].

Raebeck, B. (1999). Structuring middle schools for brain-compatible learning. *Principal, 79*, 48-49.

Schiller, P. B. (1999). *Start smart.* Beltsville, MD: Gryphon House.

Stephens, K. (1999). Primed for learning: The young child's mind. *Child Care Information Exchange*, 44-48.

Sylwester, R. (1998). Art for the brain's sake. *Educational Leadership, 56*, 31-35.

Thompson, W. J. (1998). A moving science lesson. *Science and Children, 36*, 24-27.

Tomlinson, C. A., & Kalbfleisch, M. L. (1998). Teach me, teach my brain: A call for differentiated classrooms. *Educational Leadership, 56*, 52-55.

Weikart, P. S. (1998). Facing the challenge of motor development. *Child Care Information Exchange*, 60-62.

Assessment Alternatives

Chapter 22
Rubrics:
The Learners' Choice

Kathleen Glascott Burriss,
Middle Tennessee State University

ducators at the state, district, and class-room levels are using rubrics as effective assessment alternatives. Distinguished from other forms of assessment by detailed description, rubrics delineate a range of student performances. The purpose of this chapter is to provide classroom teachers with descriptions for using, designing, and interpreting rubrics on behalf of students' learning.

Why Use Rubrics?

Traditional educational practice has been guided by the notion that students are passive receptors with finite capacities to learn. Information, it is believed, can be transmitted through instruction, and students' learning identified by a final prod-uct. Tests are assumed to objectively measure this product and determine students' learning by quantifying correct responses. These scores have come to legitimize both student achievement and teacher accountability. Consequently, subject-driven instruction, with the intent to promote students' ability to score well on tests, drives much public school practice (Elkind, 1989).

In contrast, newer perspectives point to the evolving nature of learners' mental abilities. Although materials and instruction are important, the critical regard is for the individual learner's internal mental activity. That is, the very process of learning is integral to the knowledge being constructed. This means the demonstrated product and the process of learning cannot be separated. Knowledge cannot be transmitted.

Rather, student knowledge is understood to be personally constructed. For the nontraditional educator, the intent is to promote students' independent learning through inquiry and cre-ative expression (Brooks & Brooks, 1999; DeVries & Kohlberg, 1987; Elkind, 1989, 1991).

In an effort to meet the needs of a diverse student population, teachers are exploring innova-tive ways to build upon learners' personal histo-ries. This shift away from subject-driven teaching is described as reflective, holistic, child-centered, constructive, developmental, or authentic (Zemelman, Daniels, & Hyse, as cited in Richards & Cheek, 1999). As teachers move away from traditional teaching and learning methods, class-rooms will begin to look and sound different. In order to maintain learning integrity, different methods of instruction warrant different means of assessment. Thus, the key to effective evaluation is to appropriately match the assessment tool with the learning task (Burke, 1999).

For the purposes of this discussion, learning will be related to performance tasks, which in turn can be assessed through "rubrics."

What Is a Performance Task?

Performance tasks refer to assessments in which students are expected to construct an original response (Popham, 1999). Unlike traditional assignments, performance tasks integrate several skills and attempt to resemble real-life experiences (Burke, 1999; Popham, 1999). Students not only understand subject matter, but also are expected to apply skills and interpret information (Burke, 1999). In doing so, students are provided choices that vary according to the assignment. In turn, the teacher makes evaluative inferences from observing students' performance tasks (Popham, 1999).

Gronlund (cited in Burke, 1999) describes performance tasks as restricted or extended. Restricted refers to tasks that are highly structured and target a specific instructional objective (i.e., read an identified selection aloud or design a collage using materials prescribed by the teacher). The extended task is less structured and more comprehensive with numerous instructional objectives (writing a proposal, collecting and interpreting data). Smaller tasks also may be included, and assessed separately (Burke, 1999).

Performance tasks provide a systematic means to assess skills and procedural knowledge that is not possible in multiple-choice formats (Burke, 1999). Choosing performance tasks that are generalizable allows teachers to make the strongest performance-based inferences regarding students' capabilities (Popham, 1999).

In addition to generalizability, whether choosing from existing performance tasks or creating new ones, Popham (1999) suggests several other evaluative criteria:

- Authenticity—task is similar to what students will encounter in the real world
- Multiple foci—task measures multiple instructional outcomes
- Teachability—instructions promote students' proficiency
- Fairness—performance outcomes are not biased by students' personal characteristics
- Feasibility—task is realistically balanced with cost, space, time, and equipment
- Scorability—task produces student responses that can be reliably and accurately evaluated.

Although all of these factors are important, Popham (1999) concedes that authenticity and multiple foci may be difficult to apply in some instances.

Performance tasks represent the complexity and depth required for students' deeper understanding of a few key concepts (Burke, 1999). The notion "less is more" binds the performance task for greatest efficiency (p. 83). After describing the performance task, the teacher identifies several criteria, as outlined below.

Criteria selection is critical because these are the standards that define student adequacy (Burke, 1999; Popham, 1999; Taggart, Phifer, Nixon, & Wood, 1999). These criteria elicit particular information, which ultimately determines the value, quality, and effectiveness of student learning outcomes (Taggart et al., 1999).

What Are Rubrics?

Rose (1990) describes rubrics as a way to organize and interpret the data teachers naturally observe and gather in the course of a day. As a scoring guide, rubrics describe specific and measurable criteria that clarify proficiency levels for particular areas/behaviors (Richards & Cheek, 1999; Rose, 1990). Performance assessment is based on students' constructed-response measurement procedures (Popham, 1999). This means students generate, rather than select, responses. Although more difficult than traditional forms of evaluation, students' constructed-responses *can* be scored.

Words Detail Each Criterion

Simkins (1999) provides guidelines to support teachers' discretion when designing rubrics, the purpose of which is to be neither too specific nor too broad. In addition, he suggests the teacher prioritize and include only those details critical to evaluating the students' performance. He further advises teachers to use only four or five high points of the task per rubric and to provide each aspect with measurable and teachable criteria.

Simkins (1999) also cautions against the use of relative terms (i.e., "poor," "average," "good") because such labels do not provide the details to delineate a standard. In addition, students may become discouraged when identified with emotionally laden terms. Students require specific feedback that informs instruction.

Simkins (1999) recommends four-level rubrics; three-level rubrics do not provide the distinction between performance standards and five or more levels become overly minute. A numerical scale may be associated with each criterion. In turn, points may be assigned with verbal descriptors (Popham, 1999). If labels *must* identify levels, students can choose descriptors that are fun and relevant. If the intent is to promote an individual student's performance, comparative words like "outstanding," "good," "satisfactory," and "needs improvement" are not important.

By allowing students to participate in designing and adapting rubrics (Richards & Cheek, 1999; Simkins, 1999; Taggart et al., 1999), learning expectations are clarified and students become personally invested in their learning. Self-monitoring allows students to analyze their own attitudes, efforts, and learning processes so that they can use that knowledge to further their own learning. They reflect on their own work to determine what they have done well and what they could do better (Richards & Cheek, 1999).

Being involved in the evaluative process provides students with time to ask questions and develop personal expectations (Taggart et al., 1999). In addition, student participation diminishes the risks associated with the learning experience. Rubrics may be written individually, with a group, or with parents (Richards & Cheek, 1999).

The classroom teacher first decides on a performance task, a general description of the task that includes the instructional goals to be mastered. Next, the teacher, with student input, identifies and describes criteria that determine a range of performance levels. For example:

Performance Task: Second-graders (in groups of two) create and, using puppets, present a story to the class.
Goals: To effectively develop and orally communicate the elements of story.
(See Figure 1.)

PROMOTING A STORY WITH PUPPETS

	0	1	2	3
Story	Limited evidence	Evidence of beginning and ending of story	Evidence of beginning, middle, and end of story; some plot development	Complete story; clear plot development; resolution of conflict
Characters	0-1 character	Some character development; some dialogue	Several characters identified; meaningful dialogue	Rich character development; interactive dialogue
Communication	Puppet actions in isolation; story not related to puppets	Characters tell story	Audience appeal; story told with inflection	High audience appeal; use appropriate inflection; coordinate voice with actions
Stage	Appropriate size and lighting	Puppets represent characters; related stage background	Puppets represent characters speaking	Puppets, stage, and props contribute to story

Figure 1

Performance Task: Fourth-graders (in groups of three) create a school-wide bulletin board depicting the monthly theme.

Goals: To create an effective visual display using graphics and words appropriate to audience. (See Figure 2.)

A Different Interpretation

Rubrics, like other assessment alternatives, do not provide a final evaluative solution. Regardless of the subject matter, an assessment repertoire is needed to measure both the specific learning and the application of information and skills (Burke, 1999). Considering the time and effort it takes to design and implement rubrics, they remain only as effective as the human intervention provides. Recalling the premise for using performance task and rubrics is critical to ensuring learners' satisfaction.

Performance tasks and rubrics provide students with choices to demonstrate inquiry and creative expression. These independent learning indicators ought not be defined as "correct" or "incorrect." Instead, as described here, performance tasks and rubrics assume a developmental and instructional function. This means the intent is not to fail or undermine students' efforts. Rather, the rubric narrative provides guidelines for students' self-monitoring and teacher feedback. The additional time and effort needed for evaluating performance tasks and rubrics are best spent on behalf of long-term student learning and enhanced teacher instruction.

USING BULLETIN BOARDS TO PROMOTE THINKING

	0	1	2	3
Focus	Collection of visuals; theme not clear	Some evidence of theme	School-wide theme identified	Clearly identifies school-wide and community theme
Organization	Visual and text provided	Purposeful; visually defined; text included	Text and graphics provided	Text and graphics support the focus; school-wide and community appeal
Content	Some information provided	Some information; effort to relate text and graphics	Relevant and engaging graphics; text supports focus	Research evidenced; relevant and engaging graphics; text supports theme; school-wide and community appeal
Materials	One source	Two or more sources	Graphics and text evidence relevant design patterns; school-wide appeal	Text and graphics used in unique ways to promote understanding of school and community theme

Figure 2

From this perspective, the *process* of learning is a critical component of the *assessment* of learning. By using rubrics, teachers have the opportunity to discern individual learning styles (Taggart et al., 1999). This knowledge informs teacher instruction as the learning process continues. Independent learners, less concerned with competing with others, mark their progress with personal benchmarks (Taggart et al., 1999).

Although students participate in rubric design, comprehension is not ensured. This is particularly true when students are first introduced to performance tasks and rubrics. Different from traditional practice, rubrics and performance tasks place the responsibility for learning on the student. This shift away from subject-driven learning involves trust, and will take time and practice for both students and teachers. As a beginning, Burke (1999) recommends designing fun rubrics (e.g., a classroom party with criteria describing food, games, decorations, surprises).

Rubrics do not replace the critical importance of the teacher-student dynamic, and students' self-monitoring is done only with the continued support of the classroom teacher. In addition to timely, nonjudgmental feedback, this support includes a teacher's warmth, respect, and acceptance of students' efforts and abilities (Kostelnik, Stein, Whiren, & Soderman, 1993).

The strength of using rubrics resides in the potential to promote students' abilities to develop knowledge and apply skills across situations. It is not difficult to translate the narrative descriptors of a rubric into number and/or letter grades. Considering the time and effort involved for both teacher and student, the primary purpose for using perfor-mance tasks and rubrics is not to evaluate subject matter or single skill application. Rather, rubrics, as described, are intended to maximize individual students' efforts and capabilities. Rubrics highlight the process and not the final product. As Brooks and Brooks (1999) argue, assessment and teaching can merge into service for the learner. Rubrics, designed and interpreted appropriately, provide the link to inform practice on behalf of the learner.

References

Brooks, J. G., & Brooks, M. G. (1999). *In search of under-standing: The case for constructivist classrooms.* Alexandria, VA: Association for Supervision and Curriculum Development.

Burke, K. (1999). *The mindful school: How to assess authentic learning.* Arlington Heights, IL: SkyLight Professional Development.

DeVries, R., & Kohlberg, L. (1987). *Constructivist educa-tion: Overview and comparison with other programs.* Washington, DC: National Asociation for the Education of Young Children.

Elkind, D. (1989). Developmentally appropriate practice: Philosophical and practical implications. *Phi Delta Kappan, 71*(2), 113-117.

Elkind, D. (1991). *Perspectives on early childhood education: Growing with young children toward the 21st century.* Washington, DC: National Education Association.

Kostelnik, M., Stein, L., Whiren, A. P., & Soderman, A. (1993). *Guiding children's social development.* Albany, NY: Delmar Publishers.

Popham, W. J. (1999). *Classroom assessment: What teachers need to know.* Boston: Allyn and Bacon.

Richards, D., & Cheek, E. (1999). *Designing rubrics for K-6 classroom assessment.* Norwood, MA: Christopher-Gordon Publishers.

Rose, M. (1990). Make room for rubrics. *Instructor, 108*(2), 30-31.

Simkins, M. (1999, August). Designing great rubrics. *Technology & Learning, 20,* 23-29.

Taggart, C. E., Phifer, S. J., Nixon, J. A., & Wood, M. (1999). *Rubrics: A handbook for construction and use.* Lancaster, PA: Technomic.

Chapter 23
Portfolios

Sandra J. Stone,
Northern Arizona University

ortfolios represent authentic or performance-based, non-graded assessments that document a child's successful learning and what he can do on his own developmental continuum. Typically, portfolios are housed in a notebook or expanded folder and represent children's progress in one or all areas of growth, such as academic, social, emotional, and even aesthetic and physical development.

Portfolios clearly depart from traditional thought regarding evaluation and assessment. Many schools continue in the traditional practice of curriculum-centered evaluation, which includes high-stakes assessments, standardized tests, and grades. Wolf, LeMahieu, and Erish (1992) aptly express this practice as using "test data to rank, rather than improve, schools and to sort, rather than educate, children" (p. 9). Unfortunately, the byproducts of this type of rigid system are test-driven instruction and grades as rewards and punishments for school performance. The search for understanding, ownership of knowledge, and the joy of true learning become obscured and demeaned (Brooks & Brooks, 2000).

Portfolio assessment is one of the foundational pieces of many restructured schools, which choose to embrace learning as a constructive process and implement practices that truly help children. An understanding of human development and the cognitive sciences (e.g., constructivism) guides not only assessment practices, but also authentic teaching. The goal of deep understanding becomes the priority for establishing meaningful learning environments and assessments, rather than test-driven curricula and the superficial grade on an often low-order, fact-driven test. Assessments represented in portfolios are an ongoing and integrated part of every child's learning. The data collected is used to benefit children rather than simply test, rank, and sort them.

Teachers have found that traditional forms of assessment give an impersonal and narrow view of the child in the learning process. Portfolios give a clearer picture of what children have learned. Thus, teachers have begun to consider portfolios as more valid indicators of a child's progress, with the added bonus that they actually support children as they learn.

The following summarizes the differences between portfolio assessment and traditional assessment:

Portfolio Assessment . . .
- Uses multiple forms of assessment
- Gives a more complete picture of child's learning
- Makes assessment within contexts
- Is child-centered
- Is ongoing
- Supports the process of learning
- Focuses on what children can do
- Evaluates child's past achievements and own potential
- Benefits children by supporting their growth
- Provides teachers information to extend children's learning
- Provides opportunity for child to evaluate own learning

Traditional Assessment
- Uses one form of assessment
- Gives narrow view of child's learning
- Makes assessment in contrived learning context (i.e., test)

- Is curriculum-centered
- Conducts one-time test on particular task
- Represents isolated task, separate from the process of learning
- Focuses on what children cannot do
- Evaluates by comparison to norms
- Labels, sorts, ranks children
- Provides little information teacher can use to help child
- Uses only teacher evaluation

From Stone, S. J. (1995a). *Understanding portfolio assessment: A guide for parents.* Olney, MD: Association for Childhood Education International.

Purpose of Portfolio Assessment

The portfolio is designed to accomplish three main goals: 1) document student progress and growth, 2) support and guide instruction, and 3) communicate each student's successful growth to both child and parents (Stone, 1992, 1996).

Document student progress and growth. The pieces in the portfolio are systematically and purposefully selected to show a child's growth in the processes of learning over time. Portfolios are not mere work folders of dittos and worksheets, nor are they just a collection haphazardly thrown together.

The portfolio tells a story of what the child is learning and how the child learns. The portfolio also identifies the direction the child needs to go next in the learning process. Just as parents will document when their child first sits up, stands,

and then walks, the portfolio documents the child's steps in becoming a reader, writer, and problem solver. For example, the portfolio may document how a child progresses from writing random letters, to writing letters for sounds, and then writing words with all the syllables present (see Figure 1). Finally, the child writes using sentences and conventional spelling (Stone, 1997).

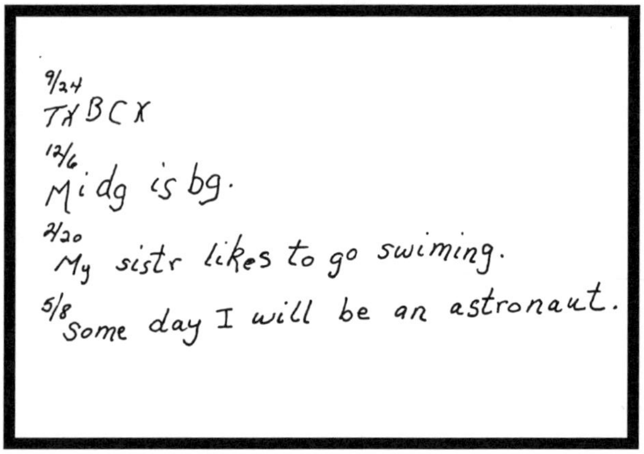

The portfolio also may document how the child first progresses from writing sentences without descriptive words, to writing with limited descriptive words, and finally to writing sentences with well-selected adverbs and adjectives (see Figure 2).

In math, the portfolio may show how a younger child understands numbers. The child may progress from using tally marks to count, to using numbers to represent quantity, to finally using numbers to add quantities (see Figure 3).

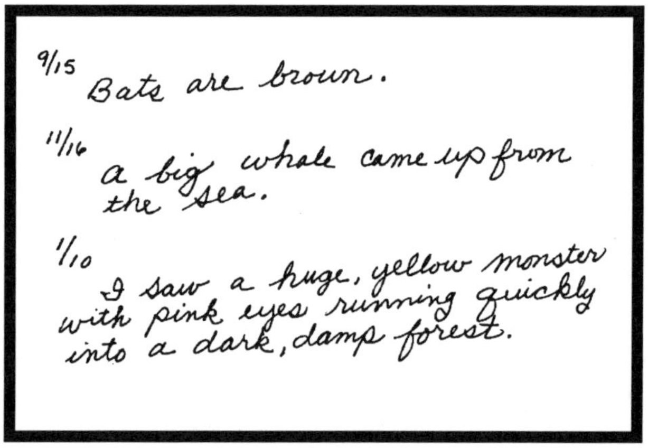

Figure 2

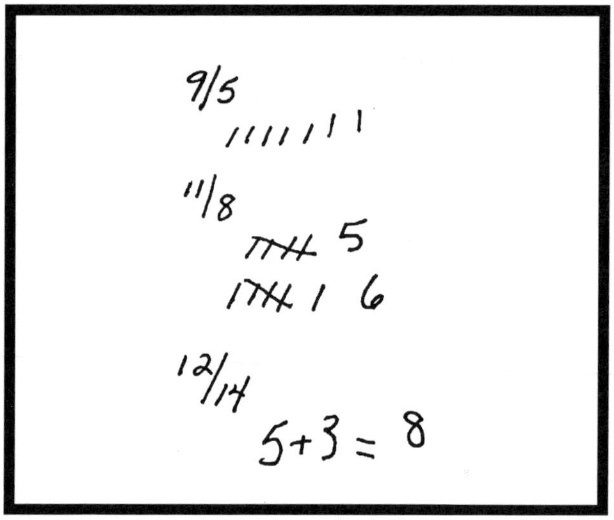

Figure 1

Figure 3

An older child may demonstrate his growth in understanding multiplication by using skills in real-life situations. The portfolio may show his growth from at first adding numbers, to grouping numbers and adding, and finally to grouping numbers and multiplying (see Figure 4).

Portfolios show the process through which a child goes in order to write a story, reach a decision, form a hypothesis, or solve a problem. With portfolios, the emphasis is on performance. What can the child do? What does the child understand? How does the child think? In portfolio assessment, the child demonstrates his ability to use skills and understand concepts. No standardized test, textbook test, or teacher-made test can provide as much important information about how the child builds his knowledge of reading, writing, and problem solving. Testing can offer only a product, a score, with no evidence of how the child produced the product or if the child understands what he or she is learning. The portfolio shows the process a child goes through when becoming a reader, writer, scientist, or mathematician.

Support and guide instruction. In all the preceding examples, the teacher is actively involved in using daily portfolio assessments to guide her instructional practice in order to help each child continue to grow in his or her knowledge and skills. The portfolio documents where the child is in the learning process; this knowledge helps the teacher assess the child's needs and then select the most appropriate instructional strategies to help the child go on to the next successful step. For example, a child may be reading at a frustrational level in a guided reading group. The teacher, who is making daily assessments with the tool of a running record, can immediately make a decision to change the level of the reading text in order to promote the child's successful reading development. In another example, if a child is consistently and independently solving math problems, the teacher uses the assessment tools to move the child on to more challenging work (Stone, 1995b). Portfolios, used as dynamic, interactive instructional tools, empower teachers in their instructional decision making (DeFina, 1992; Herman & Winters, 1994; Stone, 1995b).

Communicate each student's successful growth to both child and parents. As children become involved in the portfolio process, they will begin to see themselves as successful learners. The portfolio vividly portrays to them their competence, success, and self-worth, and compels them to keep involved in the learning process. Portfolios also help parents focus on their children's strengths, not weaknesses. They are able to have a more complete picture of their children's learning and can celebrate their successes.

What's in a Portfolio?

A portfolio contains purposefully selected pieces. These pieces most often represent a child's learning process in academic areas, but also can include evidence of the child's social, emotional, aesthetic, and physical development. The following items may be placed in a child's portfolio:

Performance-based and authentic-based assessments. Teachers may use two kinds of assessments to place in the portfolio: performance-based and authentic-based. In performance-based assessments, the context is pre-determined. The teacher will give the same assessment to all the students, usually at the beginning, middle, and end of the year. This allows the teacher to see each child's

Figure 4

147

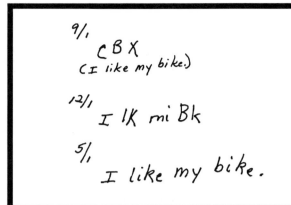

Figure 5

measures such as a multiple-choice test, in which the child simply selects correct answers.

Sample Performance-based Assessments
- Letter Recognition
- Sentence Dictation
- Vocabulary Assessment
- Concepts of Print
- Running Records
- Math Facts

Sample Authentic-based Assessments
- Writing Samples
- Problem-solving Examples
- Retellings
- Literature Logs
- Science/Social Studies Projects
- Integrated Curriculum Projects
- Open-ended Learning Centers
- Plays

growth and understanding over time within the same context.

For example, the teacher may dictate several sentences to a child at the beginning of the year in order to investigate the child's understanding of the sound-symbol relationship. She would then dictate the same sentences at the middle and end of the year (see Figure 5).

Another pre-determined context may be for performance in math. Children are assessed on multiplication tables at the beginning, middle, and end of the year with the same assessment. The teacher will look for growth in each child's ability to use multiplication facts as it develops throughout the year. The teacher will use the pre-determined criteria to evaluate progress.

Authentic-based assessment also is based on a child's performance. In authentic assessment, however, the context is not pre-determined. Authentic assessment includes actual examples of work that the child has performed as part of the ongoing work and activity of the classroom. For example, a teacher may select a journal page from a child's reflection on a science experiment. At the beginning of the year, the child's work may demonstrate some understanding of the science process skills, while a later sample may demonstrate a more complete understanding, thus documenting growth. Both performance-based and authentic-based assessments rely on demonstrations of what the child can actually do in an authentic context, rather than on less genuine

Checklists. A checklist is a summary of skills, which reflects a child's growth developmentally. A checklist is a quick way to see where the child is and where the child should be going next. Teachers often use checklists for reading, writing, and math (see Figure 6).

Anecdotal records. Anecdotal records are observations of a child's performances recorded by the teacher while observing or working with the child. The teacher observes the child engaged in meaningful classroom experiences and gathers information about the child's strengths, interests, strategies, and needs. Anecdotal records give the teacher insight into the child's academic, social, and emotional development.

Example:
1/21   Jason writes mostly with capital letters
2/12   Jason is now writing correctly with appropriate capital and lowercase letters

Vignettes. While similar to anecdotal records, vignettes are more detailed accounts of a significant understanding for the child. Usually, the teacher writes vignettes after, rather than during, the observation.

Example:

This morning Sarah displayed her first understanding of the concept of writing a hypothesis. In the weeks prior to this, Sarah was baffled. She would write a statement or definition, but couldn't generate the questions that accompany a hypothesis. In her project today, I could see not only her understanding of how to develop a hypothesis, but also the "follow through" in proving it. She even spent some of her time helping her friend, Maria, work on her hypothesis. This is where I found the depth of her understanding, as she explained the process to Maria.

Student self-evaluations. In portfolio assessment, students are invited to reflect on their own work and progress. Students also may include goals for future progress. These reflections and goals are included in the portfolio.

Example:

In my narrative, I showed that I can write with describing words. My goals are to write with more describing words and use paragraphs.

Information from questionnaires, interviews, and conferences. Teachers also may include information from questionnaires in a child's portfolio. Questionnaires often give information on a child's interests or dispositions.

Example:

1. What is your favorite book?
2. How do you feel about reading?

A teacher also may include interviews or conferences with the child. In an interview, the teacher may ask the child to explain his understanding of place value, or his interests for an upcoming science project. Information from a teacher-child conference may reflect what the child knows and guide the teacher or child in future goals.

Parent observations and conferences. Parents may fill out questionnaires or supply information during conferences regarding their child's interests, needs, and strengths, providing insights that may not be apparent to the teacher. Together, parents and teachers can effectively support a child's growth, both at home and at school, and document it in a portfolio.

Photographs, audiotapes, and videotapes. Photographs and videotapes can capture certain strengths of a child that cannot be fully captured on paper, such as a child building a simple machine, painting a mural, or participating in a play. An audiotape can document a child's reading ability and expression over time.

Peer reviews. Children can review and evaluate each other's work, offering helpful suggestions. In the process, they become better critics of their own work. During the peer review process, children have the added benefit of seeing their work being valued by others.

Who Decides What Goes Into a Portfolio?

With the goals of documenting progress, guiding instruction, and communicating a child's successful growth, both the teacher and child make decisions about what goes into the portfolio. Parents are also invited to participate with supportive comments about their child's growth and development, and to provide evidential artifacts.

What's a Portfolio Conference?

For the teacher and children. Teachers have conferences with individual students on a regular basis. It is during these conferences that the teacher and child discuss the child's progress. The teacher praises the child for his successes and helps him set goals for the next growth step. For example, the teacher may ask the child to evaluate a piece of writing, asking, "Are you using periods and spaces?" or "Are you using adverbs?" As children become thoughtful evaluators of their own work, the teacher documents progress and uses the information to design her instruction. Such conferences tend to last only a few minutes and occur during the course of daily instruction. Conferences allow both children and teachers to understand each other and to collaborate for the benefit of the child (Stone, 1996).

For the teacher, parents, and children. Portfolio conferences for both parents and children usually occur quarterly, often taking the place of the

READING DEVELOPMENT
CHECKLIST

Name _____ Date _____

STAGE ONE	SEP	OCT	NOV	DEC	JAN	FEB	MAR	APR	MAY
Front/back of book									
Top/bottom of page									
Attends to pictures: Labels/comments									
Attends to pictures: Tells story									
Print contains meaning									
Differentiates letters/words									
Concept of word/space									
Identifies some environmental print									
One-to-one matching (voice to print)									
Knows where to begin									
Left-to-right/Return sweep									
Memorizes text									
STAGE TWO	SEP	OCT	NOV	DEC	JAN	FEB	MAR	APR	MAY
Attends to some print									
Identifies some letters									
Identifies sight words									
Uses picture clues									
Uses familiar story									
Uses beginning consonants									
Uses beginning and end consonants									
Uses some strategies (mean., syn., phon.)									
Expects reading to make sense									
Expects reading to sound right									
Uses knowledge of letter/sound relationships									
Takes risks without fear of making errors									
STAGE THREE	SEP	OCT	NOV	DEC	JAN	FEB	MAR	APR	MAY
Reads using all strategies (mean., syn., phon.)									
Uses decoding to confirm or disconfirm other strategies									
Self-corrects									
Rereads for meaning									
Reads on to gain meaning									
Retells story (set., char., theme, plot, res.)									
STAGE FOUR	SEP	OCT	NOV	DEC	JAN	FEB	MAR	APR	MAY
Reads with fluency (expression, rate)									
Silently reads new text independently									
Integrates all strategies (mean., syn., phon.)									
Reads different ways for different purposes									
Comprehends text (literal, inferential, critical)									

Figure 6

MATH DEVELOPMENT
CHECKLIST 1
Ages 5-8

Name _____ Date_____

NUMBER AND NUMERATION	SEP	OCT	NOV	DEC	JAN	FEB	MAR	APR	MAY
One-to-One Correspondence									
Equivalent Sets									
Using Numerals (1-10, 1-20, 1-100)									
Counting (1-10, 1-20, 1-100)									
Counting to 100 (by 2's, by 5's, by 10's)									
Writing Numerals (1-10, 1-20, 1-100)									
Ordering Numerals (1-10, 1-20, 1-100)									
Number Lines									
Ordinal Numbers (1st-3rd, 1st-5th, 1st-12th)									
Set and Subset									
More than; Less than									
Odd and Even Numbers									
Reading and Writing Numerals									
Place Value (3 digits, 4 digits, 5 digits)									
Round Off (10's, 100's, 1000's)									
Estimation									
Roman Numerals									
OPERATIONS OF WHOLE NUMBERS	SEP	OCT	NOV	DEC	JAN	FEB	MAR	APR	MAY
Addition (Sums through 5, 10, 20)									
Associative Property of Addition									
Column Addition									
(Two digit, Three digit, Four digit)									
(Two digit w/regrouping, Three digit w/regrouping)									
Subtraction									
(One digit, Two digit, Three digit)									
Commutative Property of Subtraction									
(Two digit w/regrouping, Three digit w/regrouping)									
Commutative Property of Multiplication									
Multiplication (Basic Facts: 1-5, 6-10, 11-12)									
(Relation to Addition)									
(One digit, Two digit by one digit, Two digit)									
Division (Basic Facts: 2-3, 4-6, 7-9)									
(Relation to Multiplication)									
(Estimating Quotients)									

Figure 6, continued

traditional report card or accompanying a narrative report card. During the conference, parents and child review the contents of the portfolio, reviewing the child's successes. The child's strengths, rather than weaknesses, are the focal point. Parents, teachers, and the child all have an opportunity to celebrate the child's progress, exchange information, and set goals (Stone, 1996).

Parents are finding that they know much more about their children from portfolios than from the traditional approach of tests and grades. Parents like being able to see what their children can do, such as write a story, plan a science experiment, or solve a real problem. Parents appreciate the personal and individual attention their children receive through portfolio assessment.

What Are the Benefits of Portfolio Assessment?

The foundational purpose of portfolio assessment is to benefit children in the learning process.

Portfolio Assessment . . .

Respects the learning process. Learning is a continuous process and not a final product. Portfolios illustrate the process.

Respects child's individuality. With portfolios, each child is perceived as an individual on his or her own continuum of learning, rather than being compared to other children or measured according to arbitrarily set standards. While expectations are high, they reflect the child's own learning rate and style.

Documents children's growth. A portfolio shows each child's growth in the learning process. With the focus on the child's growth, each step can be celebrated as a success.

Supports a child's chance for success, competence, and self-worth. With the focus on strengths, rather than weaknesses, children can see themselves as successful, competent learners.

Encourages children to value the learning process. When children are invited to participate in their own learning and are given ownership of the process, they value learning as an exciting, positive, and personal experience. Children experience the joy of learning.

Encourages children to be thoughtful evaluators of their own work. Children are encouraged to reflect on their own work, instead of always relying on someone else to make judgments. As thoughtful evaluators of their own work, children set goals and continue learning.

Supports and guides instruction. Through portfolio assessment, the teacher knows where the child is and where he or she needs to go next. With this knowledge, the teacher can adjust instruction to meet the learning needs of each child. Instruction, then, is based on the developing needs of the children as assessed by the teacher through the portfolio, and not on material dictated by a test irrespective of the child's needs.

Increases teachers' awareness of how children learn. Through observations and by documenting growth, teachers are able to see the process by which children construct or build their knowledge. This vitally important information supports the teacher's ability to nurture each child's successful development.

Serves as a vehicle for communicating with child and parent. The portfolio is a tool for reporting the child's growth and development to the child and parent. This tool gives both the opportunity to see the child as a successful learner and to celebrate together his or her successes.

Promotes lifelong learning. When the child sees himself or herself as a competent learner, he or she is motivated to continue learning. Learning does not stop in the classroom, but continues throughout life as a reward in itself.

Above adapted from Stone, S. J. (1996). *Creating the multiage classroom.* Parsippany, NJ: Good Year Books. Used by permission.

References

Brooks, J. G., & Brooks, M. G. (2000). *In search of understanding: The case for constructivist classrooms.* Alexandria, VA: Association for Supervision and Curriculum Development.

DeFina, A. A. (1992). *Portfolio assessment: Getting started.* New York: Scholastic.

Herman, J. L., & Winters, L. (1994). Portfolio research: A slim collection. *Educational Leadership, 52*(2), 48-55.

Stone, S. J. (1992). Portfolio assessment—Beneficial for

children's growth. *Focus on Early Childhood, 5,* 1-4.

Stone, S. J. (1995a). *Understanding portfolio assessment: A guide for parents.* Olney, MD: Association for Childhood Education International.

Stone, S. J. (1995b). Portfolios: Interactive, dynamic instructional tool. *Childhood Education, 71,* 232-234.

Stone, S. J. (1996). *Creating the multiage classroom.* Parsippany, NJ: Good Year Books.

Stone, S. J. (1997). Using portfolios to assess and nurture early literacy from a developmental perspective. In K. B. Yancey & I. Weiser (Eds.), *Situating portfolios: Four perspectives* (pp. 163-175). Logan, UT: Utah State Press.

Wolf, D. P., LeMahieu, P. G., & Erish, J. (1992). Good measure: Assessment as a tool for education reform. *Educational Leadership, 49,* 8-13.

Chapter 24
Observations and Reflections

H. Willis Means,
Middle Tennessee State University

The Morton Umbrella Girl is one of the most enduring features of commercial advertising. Since 1914, she has appeared in a rainstorm with umbrella open, box tilted backward under her arm, and salt pouring from the opened spout. You could imagine that if you looked closely at the box she is holding, there would appear another girl, umbrella open, holding a box of salt. And on that box you would find yet another girl, umbrella open, holding a box of salt, and so on and so on. The Morton Salt slogan is "When it rains it pours"; upon reflection, however, another message, perhaps not intentional, is that it pours, and pours, and pours, and pours.

When examining the connections among observation, reflection, assessment, and instruction, one is reminded of the Morton Umbrella Girl: The more you look, the more you see; the more you reflect, the more explanations you generate to explain what was observed; the more you modify your instruction to assess the validity of the explanations, the more you look. . . .

Schön (1983, 1987) identifies four types of reflection that may be used in a classroom: 1) technical rationality, 2) reflection-in-action, 3) reflection-on-action, and 4) reflection-for-action. The first, technical rationality, deals with the immediate consideration of what has occurred in a classroom. Technical rationality focuses on "application of skills and technical knowledge in the classroom" (Farrell, 1998, p. 2). Reflection-in-action concerns our thinking about what the teacher is doing in the classroom while teaching and acting on the "spur of the moment" to modify an instructional task. Reflection-on-action requires the teacher to look back upon a class or incident and reflect on what occurred (Schön, 1987); while this may incorporate reflection-in-action, it differs in that the teacher is attempting to discover how or why something happened (Farrell, 1998). Finally, reflection-for-action requires the teacher to be proactive and "undertake reflection, not so much to revisit the past or to become aware of the meta cognitive processes one is experiencing . . . but to guide future action" (Killon & Todnew, 1991, p. 15).

Observation: Reflection-in-Action

Observation is probably the most common informal assessment measure used by teachers. Teachers, by definition, are observers. The word "pedagogue" comes from the Greek "paidagogos," the name given to the slave who led and observed a child on the way to and from school each day. Today, teachers watch children on the playground, in the halls, in the lunchroom, and, of course, in the classroom. It is not uncommon to hear teachers describing a student's behavior to a colleague. Often, what teachers take for granted during their observations can be used systematically to improve instruction.

Observational assessment affords the teacher at least two advantages over more formal assessment measures (McLoughlin & Lewis, 1990). First, they are unobtrusive. Observational assessment is part of what teachers do every day. Children will not think it unusual that their teacher is watching them as they work, play, or interact with each other. Second, observation can be done regardless of a

155

student's age, the instructional setting, or curriculum area.

There are at least four ways to conduct observational assessments: 1) informal observation and anecdotal records, 2) interviews and student reflections, 3) checklists and rating systems, and 4) teacher questions (Gredler, 1999). Each has strengths and weaknesses; when used in combination with other informal and formal assessment measures, each can contribute to a more complete description of an incident than is possible with an assessment measure used in isolation (McLoughlin & Lewis, 1994).

Informal Observation and Anecdotal Records

Informal observations and anecdotal records are among the most frequently used observational assessment measure. They may be used to keep track of a student's behaviors, work habits, interests, motivation, interactions with peers, problem-solving abilities, learning style, and organization skills, in addition to the obvious focus areas of strengths and weaknesses (Gill, n.d.). The value of informal observation lies in its unobtrusiveness—all that is required is some way to keep a record of what is observed.

Recording what is observed is critical. While it is not necessary to record the observation at the immediate time it was made, the incident should be recorded as soon as possible to minimize the effect of time on one's recollection. These field notes permit the teacher to "freeze the event in time" (Harker, 1985, p. 226) and provide a record of behaviors and development, as well as general impressions of a classroom over a period of time (Hopkins, 1993). They enable the teacher to focus on a particular behavior (student's or teacher's), consider its effects, and then revisit the incident for further analysis and reflection.

A problem associated with this type of assessment is the amount of information that will be generated. Observation, by its nature, generates a great deal of information. Unless the teacher determines, in advance, the focus of the observation, information overload will occur—the inability to see the forest for the trees. It is essential to

determine the focus of the observation before starting to observe the quality of a student's work on a variety of assignments, interaction in a reading group, behavior at a center, or the effect of a schedule change on student achievement. The more narrow the focus of the observation, the more likely one is to identify specific behaviors and the more beneficial the data will be when reflecting on what was observed. Narrowing the focus of the observation also minimizes the tendency to "rush to judgment." Informal observation requires patience. A narrowly focused observation will require several observations to gather enough data to begin reflection; this delay, in turn, minimizes the tendency to reach a decision based not on what was observed, but rather on personal theories or intuition (Hopkins, 1993).

Another problem associated with informal observation and anecdotal records is the time required to keep the observations current. An obvious solution is to keep a notepad handy and jot down an impression or a descriptive word or two and then expand upon them later. An alternative to the notepad are Post-it notes, which may be inserted into the appropriate area of the field notes for future reference.

Conducting informal observations and keeping anecdotal records are time-intensive activities and require advance planning. Nevertheless, teachers who have used either or both of these methods report that they often see things they had not seen before in their classroom, and have noticed things about their students' learning they had not noticed earlier (Gomez, Graue, & Bloch, 1991; Lamme & Hysmith, 1991).

Interviews and Student Reflections

Through student interviews, teachers can obtain information about student progress, clarify their thinking about the student's abilities, further an understanding of changes in a student's work or behavior, or obtain information about a student's attitude or perception toward a subject or activity (Gredler, 1999). Traditionally, such interviews are conducted one-on-one and usually consist of several oral questions designed to elicit clarifications or probe a student's thinking. However, this does not have to be the case. Interviews also may be done in writing at the end of a unit or as an end-of-week activity. If done in writing, the student may be asked to reflect on a series of questions, such as: "What have I learned this week about how I learn best?" "What did I do in class this week that surprised me?" "Of everything I did in class this week, what one thing would I do differently?" "What did I do in class this week of which I am most proud?" "What class activities this week were the hardest for me?" "Which class activities were the easiest?" (Brookfield, 1995, pp. 97-98). Students can record their responses and provide a copy for the teacher, as well as a copy for their portfolio. Weekly written interviews become a valuable and "regular source of information" (Brookfield, 1995, p. 99). The teacher learns what methodologies work and do not work, what is happening in the class, and what changes could be made to enhance learning.

Student interviews, either in person or as responses to written questions, provide teachers with valuable information about student thinking, attitudes, and perceptions; they are helpful tools for assessing academic progress. Interviews, either written or oral, provide a way for the teacher to explore, in depth, any issues, behaviors, or concerns that were previously observed.

Checklists and Rating Systems

Checklists and rating systems were developed to help enumerate the occurrences of specific behaviors and provide either descriptive or quantitative data. These checklists can be commercially developed or they can be teacher-developed and thus focus on behaviors unique to a classroom. Checklists itemize identified behaviors; the teacher simply makes a mark each time the behavior is observed. If a teacher-developed checklist is to be used, care must be taken to ensure that the behaviors are observable and do not include items that require inferential judgments (Gredler, 1999; McLoughlin & Lewis, 1994).

Rating systems, in contrast, permit inferential judgments and may incorporate a Likert-type scale. The goal of a rating system is to achieve an understanding of the directionality of a student's

behavior (e.g., the behavior occurs: always, most of the time, half of the time, occasionally, never). As observational assessment tools, rating systems are appropriate when the characteristics of the behavior being observed may be arranged on a scale (McLoughlin & Lewis, 1994).

Teacher Questions

Teacher questions follow informal observation as one of the most common informal assessment approaches in a classroom. Questioning, like observing, is something teachers seem to do naturally. Questions can assess lower-order thinking (e.g., "In what year was the Declaration of Independence signed?") or higher-order thinking (e.g., "How would your life be different today if Jack Kilby had not developed the integrated circuit?").

Questions designed to assess student understandings have assumed a more important role in the classroom as more emphasis has been placed on performance assessment. In mathematics, for example, students are expected to provide more than answers; they are expected to engage in mathematical thinking and justify their conclusions (Schoenfeld, 1992). Teachers are expected to develop lessons that foster creative problem solving and that encourage thinking and exploration (Gredler, 1999).

Student responses or non-responses to questions permit the teacher to assess a student's understanding of a concept. The teacher should not be satisfied with simple responses, but engage in further probing, asking for justification and seeking connections between ideas and concepts observed, and assessing a student's understanding (Stein, Grover, & Henningsen, 1996).

Summary

Observation is an invaluable instructional tool, as it provides the teacher with data from a variety of sources. Observation informs instruction; is unobtrusive; aids in documenting a student's progress; can be used with any student, regardless of age, instructional level, or instructional setting; and can be used to help form hypotheses facilitating reflective inquiry (Gill, n.d.; McLoughlin &

Lewis, 1994). Responses to questions can be used immediately by the teacher to modify an instructional approach (reflection-in-action) or in combination with interviews, informal observations, anecdotal records, or checklists to help determine or guide future instruction (reflection-on-action). In any case, "the key to effective teaching is building on what students have already learned. The best way to discover this is to listen and watch closely. . ." (Jaggar, 1985, p. 5).

Reflective Inquiry and Assessment; Reflection-for-Action

John Dewey (1997) defined reflective thought as "active, persistent, and careful consideration of any belief or supposed form of knowledge in the light of the grounds that support it, and the further conclusions to which it tends" (p. 6). He also identified two subprocesses that are always present when one engages in reflective thinking: "(a) a state of perplexity, hesitation, doubt, and (b) an act of search or investigation directed toward bringing to light further facts which serve to corroborate or to nullify the suggested belief" (p. 9).

Reflective thought is observation taken to a new level. Whatever the teacher has collected or recorded becomes data for reflective thought. The initial stage requires a careful examination of the data. What does it say? Are there patterns? Can you describe what went on? Did something happen more than once? This requires reading and re-reading what the data is saying. Initially, you may experience "perplexity, hesitation, [and] doubt"; if you work with the data and keep in mind your observation focus, however, the data will begin "to speak to you." It will suggest an initial solution.

One way to move beyond the "perplexity, hesitation, [and] doubt" stage is to lay all of your artifacts on the floor or on a large table. Select one and try to find a related artifact or one that may provide an explanation or add another detail. Repeat this process until you feel that you have put the artifact(s) into a context. Go back through the collection and reflect on what you have collected. Do the artifacts come from a single data source, such as

informal observation or anecdotal records? If so, do you have one or more different data sources that contribute to your understanding? Add these to your collection. What you are creating is structural corroboration; that is, you are "put[ting] together a constellation of bits and pieces of evidence that substantiate the conclusion one wants to draw" (Eisner, 1991, p. 55).

It may be that you have an idea, based on your observations or reflective thought, as to why an event occurred or a student behaved in a certain manner. If so, examine your artifacts for supporting data, being careful not to "rush to judgment" and being aware that reflective thinking "is judgment suspended during further inquiry" (Dewey, 1997, p. 13).

The next-to-last step in the process is reflection-for-action. In this step, it is necessary for you to critically reflect on what you have discovered. You have recalled experiences using a variety of informal observation measures and artifacts, you have put the artifacts in a context you have examined, and you have reflected on what the artifacts say to you. Now you are ready to formulate a plan of action. If more than one solution suggests itself, return to your data. Decide which option appears to have the best chance for success based on your data and reflective thinking. After you implement your plan of action, you begin again: reflection-in-action (observation), reflection-on-action (organizing your artifacts), and reflection-for-action (implementation).

Conclusion: Reflection-for-Action

The relationship between assessment, observation, and reflection is symbiotic. Separately, observation, reflection, and assessment are effective assessment tools; when combined, they "help teachers move from a level where they may be guided largely by impulse, intuition, or routine, to a level where their actions are guided reflection and critical thinking" (Richards, 1990, p. 5). To understand what is going on in a classroom, we have to be close observers, document what we see, question and reflect on what we observed, and develop a plan of action based on our reflective thought of what we really saw. And we have to be willing to repeat the process again, and again, and again.

References

Brookfield, S. D. (1995). *Becoming a critically reflective teacher.* San Francisco: Jossey-Bass.

Dewey, J. (1997). *How we think.* Mineola, NY: Dover.

Eisner, E. W. (1991). *The enlightened eye: Qualitative inquiry and the enhancement of educational practice.* New York: Macmillan.

Farrell, T. (1998). Reflective teaching: The principles and practices. *English Teaching Forum, 36* [on-line] http://exchanges.state.gov/forum/vols/vol36/no4/p10.htm

Gill, H. (n.d.). *Kid watching: A naturalistic assessment technique.* [on-line] www.ehhs.cmich.edu/ins/kidart.perf

Gomez, M. L., Graue, M. E., & Bloch, M. N. (1991). Reassessing portfolio assessment: Rhetoric and reality. *Language Arts, 68,* 620-628.

Gredler, M. E. (1999). *Classroom assessment and learning.* New York: Longman.

Harker, J. O. (1985). When you get the right answer to the wrong question: Observing and understanding communication in classrooms. In A. Jaggar & M. T. Smith-Burke (Eds.), *Observing the language learner* (pp. 221-231). Newark, DE: International Reading Association.

Hopkins, D. (1993). *A teacher's guide to classroom research* (2nd ed.). Buckingham, UK: Open University Press.

Jaggar, A. M. (1985). On observing the language learner: Introduction and overview. In A. Jaggar & M. T. Smith-Burke (Eds.), *Observing the language learner* (pp. 1-7). Newark, DE: International Reading Association; Urbana, IL: National Council of Teachers of English.

Killon, J., & Todnew, G. (1991). A process of personal theory building. *Educational Leadership, 46,* 14-16.

Lamme, L., & Hysmith, C. (1991). One school's adventure into portfolio assessment. *Language Arts, 68,* 629-640.

McLoughlin, J. A., & Lewis, R. (1994). *Assessing special students.* New York: Merrill.

Richards, J. (1990). Beyond training: Approaches to teacher education in language teaching. *Language Teacher, 14,* 3-8.

Schoenfield, A. H. (1992). Learning to think mathematically: Problem solving, metacognition, and sense making in mathematics. In D. A. Grouws (Ed.), *Handbook of research on mathematics teaching and learning* (pp. 334-370). New York: Macmillan.

Schön, D. A. (1983). *The reflective practitioner.* New York: Basic Books.

Schön, D. A. (1987). *Educating the reflective practitioner: Toward a new design for teaching and learning in the professions.* San Francisco: Jossey-Bass.

Stein, M. K., Grover, B. W., & Henningsen, M. (1996). Building student capacity for mathematical thinking and reasoning: An analysis of mathematical tasks used in reform classrooms. *American Educational Research Journal, 33,* 455-488.